transitional

transitional

IN ONE WAY OR ANOTHER,
WE ALL TRANSITION

munroe
bergdorf

TONIC

LONDON · OXFORD · NEW YORK · NEW DELHI · SYDNEY

BLOOMSBURY TONIC
Bloomsbury Publishing Plc
50 Bedford Square, London, WC1B 3DP, UK
29 Earlsfort Terrace, Dublin 2, Ireland

BLOOMSBURY, BLOOMSBURY TONIC and the Bloomsbury Tonic logo are
trademarks of Bloomsbury Publishing Plc

First published in Great Britain 2023

A catalogue record for this book is available from the British Library

ISBN: HB: 978-1-5266-3031-5; TPB: 978-1-5266-3033-9; EBOOK: 978-1-5266-3034-6;
EPDF: 978-1-5266-5051-1

2 4 6 8 10 9 7 5 3 1

Typeset by Newgen KnowledgeWorks Pvt. Ltd., Chennai, India
Printed and bound in Great Britain by CPI Group (UK) Ltd, Croydon CR0 4YY

To find out more about our authors and books visit www.bloomsbury.com
and sign up for our newsletters

In Memory of Sarah Ava Fersi

Thank you for showing me the truth about love.

The love that I deserve,

The love that others deserve,

The love that I owe to myself.

I promise to live this life for the both of us.

Contents

Introduction

Sometimes, not often, but sometimes, I ask myself this question: what if I'd just done nothing? What if I'd remained stuck in purgatory between the hand I was dealt at birth and the outward lie that appeased those around me? How long could I have kept it up? What if I had just let life play out with no intervention? How long would it have taken for me to find an alternative happiness, one that would have stuck? Would happiness ever have shown its face, or would things have continued to unravel?

Who would I be now, if I hadn't started searching for who I was back then?

This isn't to say that I for one minute regret transitioning; it is the single most courageous act of self-love that I can fathom. Today I am a world apart from the shy, nervous, blank canvas of a child I once was... But it's hard not to ponder where I would have ended up if I had headed down the other fork in the road. I can't imagine the outward lie would have lasted long. I've never been very good at keeping *those* kinds of secrets. A double life never much appealed to me, especially after having to live so long as someone I wasn't. I've always been an all-or-nothing kind of girl.

I usually think these thoughts when I am my most run-down, after I've exhausted my body in trying to keep up with my mind's pace. I tend to unconsciously push myself past emotional checkpoints that I'm not physically or mentally ready for, and the thoughts usually accumulate in a wandering mind inside a burnt-out brain.

My decision to transition was a life adjustment, not a life change. We do not all of a sudden become a whole different person upon the realisation of our *transness*. None of us becomes a whole different person the moment we start presenting ourselves in a way that aligns with who we are on the inside. We do not change just because people start to see us differently from how they initially perceived us. And what struck me when I started to contemplate these ideas around my transition, was just how deeply transitioning is ingrained in our human experience. It is not a process that only trans people go through: transitioning is universal. We all do it.

Transitioning is an alignment of the invisible and the physical; it's the truth rising to the surface. I believe this to be one of the most fundamental and essential aspects of the human condition, and part of our experience as a conscious being, no matter who we are. As time goes on, we *all* develop as people, we all encounter traumas, lessons and transitional moments that not only shape us, but when contextualised and after we've healed, can bring us closer to a shared understanding that our differences unite us. We often aren't as different as we are led to believe we are.

None of us ever becomes someone else entirely – regardless of how we identify – but nor do we stay the same for ever. We all transition. It's what binds us, not what separates us. Be it through moving from childhood into adolescence, our sexuality, our gender, in our relationship with love, our racial identity or individual purpose, every aspect of our lives is in transition; and if we can apply transitional thinking to our lives, we can begin to deconstruct both the internal barriers within ourselves and the external barriers between each other. This benefits us all, both as individuals and in order to create a global consciousness.

We all worry how other people see us. And conversely, the idea that someone may not be who we perceive them to be is a narrative continually employed in our storytelling, from Shakespeare to Richard Curtis movies and from *Coronation Street* to *RuPaul's Drag Race*. But why are we so fascinated and obsessed by our human transition, why has so much time and space and creative storytelling been given to this idea of being (or not being) what meets the eye? I think it's because, when we observe someone change and evolve as a person, it makes us question how well we *really* know them. And this in turn makes us question how well we ever truly know ourselves.

I look forward to the day when people view a gender transition as no different from other socially accepted transitional narratives. For many, a transition is a coming-of-age story of sorts. It's no different from a girl becoming a woman, a boy becoming a man or an apprentice becoming a teacher. One way or another we all transition; it's merely a discovery of self – but a discovery of self with an audience of fascinated spectators, gatekeepers and non-believers.

Perhaps it's the visual element of a transgender person's transition that makes it such a difficult process for society to navigate. So many other ways in which we transition aren't as tangible. I have been made to feel like a spectacle in parts of my life and I've found this traumatising. So sometimes I ask myself: what if I'd just done nothing? What if I had just let life play out with no intervention? And the answer is, I would not have understood myself at all, because that would have been a refusal to engage with knowing myself.

This is a book about navigating difficulties, about how we all transition from trauma. You, the reader, will have done so too and you may be able to contemplate in your mind now the person you were before and after, and how you emerged changed from the mess you were in.

There is also the pressure that society puts on us to want to be someone else, to move the contents of our past safely into our subconscious. Our subconscious remains an un-ventured room in our house, containing all the difficult secrets, trauma, mistakes and loss that we just can't seem to part with, as much as we try. The human subconscious is the attic of the soul, a storage room for inconvenient truths, but it's also probably the place in our minds that understands our need and desire to continually transition in our lives. All a lot of us want to do is adjust parts of ourselves to feel comfortable living our lives, not to exist with one foot in the attic and the other in the living room.

It is crucial that every door of every room in our soul stays open. It is crucial that light and air runs throughout our house in order to keep a healthy, happy home for our soul and our psyche to live in. It has been in the most testing of times, the darkest, most impossible moments that I have learned the most about myself. My strength of character, resilience, endurance and determination are all products of intense self-work. This has involved frequently challenging myself in how I think. We all become stronger as we transition, and as we move from one point to another, closer to a place of honesty and empathy.

Adolescence

When I was a child, I often ran away from home. Sometimes I only made it as far as the end of the neighbourhood recreation ground, from which I could still see my house in what then felt like the far distance. I usually returned before anyone had the opportunity to notice or be alarmed. I was eight years old and already aware that running away was not a realistic solution to the problem of not wanting to be there. This didn't, however, prevent several future attempts at escape. As I got older the distance got further, the time got longer and the concern for my whereabouts grew.

I continued to try to run away long after leaving home. Some of these attempts almost killed me. Indeed, everything is an attempt to flee if you can't love who you are. Nowhere feels like home when it's you that you're running from. We stop trying to escape when we transition into our real selves.

★

She'd never admit to it, but my mother always liked a bit of gossip, which was a shame, as there really wasn't any with meat in our deeply uneventful corner of Essex. I grew up in Stansted Mountfitchet, a picturesque, upper-middle-class, Norman town in the south-east of England, surrounded by woodlands, nature reserves and fields. In retrospect, we probably *were* the gossip, on account of it being the 1990s, my mother being white and British and my father Black and Jamaican.

I always thought of my mother as a handsome woman. Tall, outwardly confident and bold in her demeanour, you always knew when she was in the room. Her Birmingham accent could often be heard before you saw her. With her naturally flame-red hair subtly muted with cool blonde highlights, cut into a short pixie crop that framed her high cheekbones, she had a stern facial expression that could melt away into warmth at the drop of a hat. She was unpredictable with her hardness and softness – fluidly so, uncompromisingly so. I was always aware that she didn't dress or behave like the other mums. She was, as I would put it back then, 'a tomboy, but a grown-up one'. It was what I loved most about her, that in her own unspoken way, she defied what a woman should look like and what a mother should be like.

My mother worked in marketing and my father was a carpenter by trade. They both came from working-class backgrounds and had, accordingly, worked hard to make it to this sleepy suburban town on the Hertfordshire border, with its low crime rate, its neat semis with manicured front lawns, its good schools and rolling countryside. The sense of community was such that everyone knew everyone else, and people often wouldn't lock their doors in daylight hours. Perhaps this was a symptom of everybody feeling like they knew each other's business. My parents strived to do their best by us – me and my brother, who was four years younger than me – sacrificing themselves and commuting to London to work long hours. I could see how Stansted would have been a place for an idyllic childhood for a different type of person.

★

The noun *adolescence* comes from the Latin word *adolescere*, which means 'to ripen' or 'to grow up'. Much of our experience as infants is spent soaking up information from our surroundings. We try and make sense of what we can see and we adapt quickly to fit our environment. We begin to emerge from the safety of the cocoon that was our childhood. We have not yet learned how to seek out information of our own accord and critique it from our own perspective; it is monitored by our parents in accordance with their beliefs, morals and prejudices. On reaching adolescence, however, for the first time in our short lives we are encouraged to think critically, to question the world we see around us and to learn from each other's cultures and experiences. Our own perspective is still forming, along with our vocabulary, but our instincts are there and that is where the clash between our involuntary identity – that which society seeks to make us – and our instinctive character – who we are in our element – can begin to arise.

However, in many ways, I feel that my adolescence was when I was first unmoored from my real self, from who I was before society (not just my parents) began telling me who I should and shouldn't be. The blissful, uncensored ignorance of childhood is left behind to make room for an overwhelming desire to fit in, to gain the approval of our peers, to walk the path that we are expected to walk rather than to tread one of our own.

We are all born into involuntary identities informed by all sorts of factors. These include race, class, gender and sexuality, along with the more specific demands of our parents and caregivers such as faith and politics. For example, the umbrella group for my identity could be womanhood and Blackness or being British – these are my shared identities. But my own identity would be my personal choices, feelings and the nuance within them. While I have negotiated the world a certain way because I am a woman, it is my personal responses to situations that have created me and create us all in a way which is unique.

An involuntary identity is an identity that comprises other people's assumptions of how your life will unfurl. It is the expectations of your parents, your family, your community. I think the most interesting thing about it is that it's never assumed that the child in question will be somehow in a minority. Some people have gender-reveal parties in which expectant parents announce to assorted guests the sex their child will be assigned to at birth. What is a gender-reveal party but a celebration of someone's involuntary identity, their assumed gender and people's perceptions of what that means and what that will involve, based on the genitalia that that baby is born with? I don't see these parents assuming their kid will be anything but cisgender and straight. My involuntary identity included the expectations my father had in believing he had a heterosexual son – a child he expected to share his passions and his general outlook on life.

The involuntary identity is usually made up of our parents' hopes and dreams of social assimilation and normativity. It's such an intoxicating dream that it often takes many, many years to question it, if you choose to do so at all. The first glimmers of questioning our involuntary identity come in adolescence. In many cases, this self-realisation is not pursued and one's own identity becomes the desire to meet the expectations of others.

An involuntary identity comes often from a sense of continuity, a sense of tradition. I think tradition can be very powerful – it can be a tool to bring people together through understanding the past. It can be very empowering to be plugged into a long line of tradition. I felt cheated at missing out on experiencing my father's Jamaican heritage, for example, as he wouldn't really talk about it when I was growing up, and my Blackness didn't have a place to root itself and draw power from. My father's brother's family lived in Wembley and when I was younger I'd spend a few weeks of my summer holidays with them because my parents would be working in London. It felt like a world away from Stansted; I'd be pulled up for how posh I sounded, how I didn't understand the slang my cousins used, how I didn't know the music, but on these sporadic visits to my uncle's house, I somewhat felt like I fitted in more than I did in Stansted.

Tradition can give us access to the teachings of our ancestors; it can show some of us visions of a world before colonialism. The problem with tradition arises when you start to think of it as static. To look back as a way to make sense of the world is one thing; it's another when you look back to find strict rules on how to go about things now. Getting stuck in one way of thinking, as a misguided act of respect or identity, serves no one. Again, tradition is often an assumed sense of continuity because it tends towards leaving out marginalised groups and progressive ways of thinking that lead to change.

As I entered adolescence, I began to feel and know my difference. What was once a feeling of being the odd one out became an understanding of being on the outside looking in. I started to feel more like an observer than a participant in the spaces that I was in. My difference made it hard for me to imagine what kind of person I should grow up to be without pretending that I wasn't different at all. Before that, I had imagined endless possibilities for myself. I felt like I could be or do anything.

★

In retrospect I was a bit of an odd kid, wonderfully so, but odd nonetheless. I would often become fixated with random things, collecting them to curate a world that looked like the one in my imagination. I had an extensive collection of pets. Initially I wanted to be a marine biologist, which eventually led to my wanting to become an entomologist, an obsession that I still can't believe my parents indulged me in. At one point we had two Giant African Snails, two Giant Millipedes and two Giant Stick Insects in our kitchen. Two rabbits lived in the courtyard, two gerbils in the dining room and a tank of Madagascar Hissing Cockroaches that seemed to multiply by the day. This menagerie was joined by my brother's cockatiel and the family dogs.

The insects were definitely a compromise between me and my parents: If they let me keep these oversized exotic specimens in the house, I wouldn't venture out into the garden and beyond to collect my own wild ones, keeping them in my desk drawers and in boxes under my bed (which I absolutely went through an era of doing…). One rainy afternoon when I was around the age of five, I collected a pot full of garden snails and put them in an empty metal Easter egg tin, which I proceeded to take to bed with me, falling asleep clutching it my arms. Much to the delight of the snails, it broke open in the middle of the night, resulting in my mum walking into my room in the morning to twenty-odd snails slithering over my face, in my bed and up the walls. Between this and a summer's day spent collecting all the butterflies that I could find to relocate in my bedroom, I'm sure that the carefully curated collection of insects seemed like a fair trade-off.

I know I romanticise my early childhood, since it was so important to me. My world felt expansive, not yet curtailed by reality or perceptions of reality. But by about the age of ten, the world had already tried to fit me into a narrative that wasn't my own. I'm now the patron of a trans kids' charity called Mermaids because

I understand the importance of listening to kids and encouraging them to be who they say they are. The more marginalised you are, the more diminished your possibilities seem because you grow more aware of a world that won't make space for you. Kids should be encouraged to dream big, to embrace and nurture their difference, to hold on to their magic. As a trans person, as is the case with many minorities, you often aren't encouraged to do any of these things.

As I crossed over from childhood to adolescence, I was encouraged to be more 'realistic', as if my imagination was a liability. Realism is not in fact always reality. It is often an idea of what is normal in the eyes of those with power; it is a cisgender, white, patriarchal, heteronormative, capitalist notion of what reality should look like. All civil rights movements are born out of some people's refusal to accept the reality that they are confronted with. The whole crux of every liberation movement is imagining a world in which we are not limited by our lived experiences, by our identity or by what the world around us looks like. We have to be able to dream of a world in which we can fulfil ourselves and make that a new reality. I had that understanding as a child, but adolescence was the beginning of the idea of myself slipping away.

For all its advantages and privileges, Stansted Mountfitchet had a monolithic culture. The late 1990s and early 2000s were a time when the intersections of sexuality, race and gender variance were conversations which had yet to become mainstream anywhere in the country in a positive or progressive sense. It was safe to say that they wouldn't be starting where I grew up. The only Black people I came across there were two girls who'd been adopted by a white couple. The only other Black families were found in the lower-income households who lived at the town's outskirts in council estates, made invisible by a total lack of interaction.

My mother was always extremely mindful of how we presented ourselves, and vocally so. What people thought mattered to her. She was very active in the community: we were at church on Sundays, my parents volunteered with the local Scouts and my mother was on the neighbourhood watch committee, or as I liked to call it in my teens, the curtain-twitchers' support group. Everyone was pleasant and community-minded enough on the surface of things. But I always felt like I was under surveillance. The perception of safety is something that has always fascinated me: how fragile it can be, how temporary, how open to interpretation depending on who you are, how far any difference can be held in great suspicion.

I'm not sure how young I was when I realised that being Black made me different, an object of fear and suspicion even when I was simultaneously perceived as effeminate, and therefore presumably unthreatening. But I felt it even before I could put words to it. Women would hold their handbags closer when I passed them on the street; a guard would appear near the pick'n'mix stand when I approached, keeping a watchful eye on my fingers and pockets; a neighbour wouldn't let me in to retrieve toys that had landed in her back garden, though she had no such objections to other children collecting theirs. People were waiting for me to grow into the threatening figure of their collective imaginings. I began to wonder if I was some sort of time-bomb. I was scared to become whatever they thought I would be. Shame isn't always explicitly recognisable, but looking back, I felt ashamed of my identity, my heritage, my skin.

Primary school started off feeling like a safe space for me. I looked forward to going to school, to seeing my friends, to being in an environment with other kids. To begin with, I'd made friends easily. I gravitated towards the girls; their company felt the most natural to me. But with every year that passed, I felt less and less comfortable, less sure of my footing. The other children developed a greater social awareness of the gender roles that were expected of them, and soon enough the girls stopped being friends with me because I 'wasn't a girl', and the boys in my class didn't want to be friends with me because I was 'too girly'. This was compounded by the fact that I stood out as the only visibly Black 'boy' in the entire school, out of all the pupils, teachers and staff. My brother, of course, was also Black, but he didn't stand out like me, having inherited a lighter skin tone than mine, much more like my mum, with freckles scattered across his face and with her auburn hair. Unable to articulate or even understand the growing sense of discomfort and disconnect I was feeling, my behaviour grew chaotic. I began to act out and eventually became considered a problem child. After one particularly frightening experience when I was shouted at by a classmate's homophobic mother, I began to shoplift random things: magazines I didn't want to read, sweets I wasn't interested in eating, cosmetics I couldn't use.

My piano teacher Valerie bought her husband a box of Cuban cigars for his birthday and I stole them and smoked one in the school toilet, setting off the fire alarm. I think I wanted to be caught, to get a response, even if it led, as in that case, to a lot of trouble. Brazenly smoking a stolen cigar in primary school at eight years old isn't about wanting to smoke a cigar; it's about wanting to express that something is very wrong without having the words to do it. My inability to filter my actions correlated with my inability to filter my feelings. Once it was decided at school that I was a problem child, I was blamed for things that weren't my fault, things that I didn't do. Once I was punched square in the face by a boy having a fight with another boy at school. It was so violent that my nose was fractured. I didn't go to the teachers although I was terrified and in great pain, and I tried to staunch the bleeding in the school toilets till I was eventually discovered. I knew that I'd end up being considered the instigator – and that's just what happened.

Home didn't always feel like a haven either. My only sibling and I weren't close. It didn't help that I resented how much my father appeared to prefer my brother. My father was what one might call 'traditional' – a Jamaican man from a hypermasculine culture, from a family of four brothers; he was overtly uncomfortable around the femininity that was evident in me from childhood. I lived in a state of high alert and self-censorship throughout my whole childhood. I never felt like I was the child that he wanted me to be.

On weekdays I'd come home from school an hour and a half before my father returned. I would get off the school bus and run home to make the most of this time, which often seemed that it was my only peace in the day, the only time that I could actually breathe, dance around and move my body in an uncensored way. But the moment I heard his car pull into the driveway, my anxiety would take over. He used to call me out for the feminine way I put my hands in front of my face when I laughed; or for the way I was sitting with my legs crossed and instruct me on how to sit like a man – with my legs apart, which felt alien to me.

When he was in a rare good mood, I'd vie for his attention and try to create a connection with him. But the next day, the mood would have evaporated and we'd be back to square one. This has affected the sort of relationships I have unconsciously sought out as an adult; I haven't always looked for people who would accept me for who I am, because I never thought I deserved anything more.

My mother and I had a better relationship. We also fought, but about silly things. She was firm, but usually fair, and when she wasn't it was always rooted in good intentions. I always loved the time that we had alone together. Trips to museums and crystal shops, where she would encourage me to learn more about the fossils and rocks that I so obsessively collected and carried with me, something that I still do to this day. I could tell that she wasn't afraid of my quirks, of my magic, but she was afraid of how the world would see them, how the world would treat me and what that would mean for the adult version of me.

Ours was not necessarily a house of emotional openness and transparency in which problems were aired or discussed. The decision-making happened behind closed doors; our opinions were not required. For a long time I felt a great deal of animosity towards my mother for not standing up for me more. It seemed clear to me that this was not a happy household. Of course, I don't know what really went on between my parents, and they never communicated it to me, because honest communication just wasn't our way back then.

★

Some kids can fake an identity to court the approval of their parents but I never could. My inability to fake my way through life would later be a gift. My femininity always ran too deep for me to be anything other than what I am. I have never understood why society sees femininity as a weakness – a feature that is subordinated and manipulative. It is for me the very epitome of humanity and a trait we all possess. Men who place great stock in their traditional masculinity and identify by it can often feel threatened by the powerful femininity of others as it reminds them of that part of themselves that they've learned to revile. When I was growing up, I could feel my father's disappointment in not having a 'son' that he could see himself reflected in, sharing the father–son bonding time that he missed out on with his dad, who had died when he was a child. I remember praying, wishing that a higher power could make me 'normal', someone that my dad could be proud of. I prayed endlessly that one day I could feel loved by him.

When I was nine, I wanted to do ballet. My mum was far less rigid when it came to challenging gender stereotypes. So off we went to a ballet class. That night my parents had a conversation. I listened through the walls. With the hyper-vigilance of a child who knew she was the main talking point, I grew up listening to these conversations between my parents. I couldn't hear the words but I could always hear the tone and there was nothing the tone didn't reveal. I never went to a ballet class again. I loved performance and dance; I wasn't a particularly good dancer but it felt freeing. Before I started being aware of the fact that I was effeminate, or camp, or feminine, I really embraced the movement of my body, and I was very expressive with it. As I grew older and started to be policed about how boys should behave and how they should move, dance felt less safe.

Gymnastics was deemed just about acceptable. I started a class and discovered that I was extremely flexible and could perform handstands, flips, splits, cartwheels and somersaults with ease, even though the coach would tell me off for my posture and pose. Girls and boys were encouraged to pose differently and my body language was invariably that of the girls. I soon got so good that it was decided I would attend a professional gymnasium an hour away. As my parents worked long hours, the mother of a boy in a neighbouring village would take me with her son after school.

Whenever we trained, I'd find myself looking over at the girls on the beam, at how they walked with an arched back and their shoulders pulled back. This felt natural to me but every time I arched my back, I'd be told to push my shoulders forward. The other boys would mimic the ways that I walked, they taunted me with girls' names and they'd flap their wrists in my face in a homophobic gesture. I felt unwelcome and humiliated but also deeply frustrated by not understanding why this was happening. I was experiencing homophobic abuse before I had even experienced significant sexual urges. One day I'd had enough so I pushed the boy whose mother gave me the lift to the floor. I knew doing this would mean that I wouldn't be able to come to the gym again, and that's just what happened. His mother asked me why I did it, but there was no way for me to tell her that her son was bullying me for being gay. She refused to bring me again. My parents found me a swimming team to join instead, in which I went on to compete at a national level. But despite ranking eleventh fastest in the country, my heart was never truly in it, not like it was with gymnastics. I've since found freedom in dance again as an adult. In a sense, modelling is a way for me to use my physicality in different ways, to become different characters, to move my body in ways I wouldn't ordinarily.

Having had my primary school experience soured by being picked on, I was keen and ready for high school to be a fresh start. This time it was going to be different. This was also when I started decorating my bedroom in a way that felt like it could reflect who I was on the inside. Earlier, I mainly had pictures of dinosaurs and insects on the walls. But by the time I was eleven, my bedroom was covered with tear sheets of the Spice Girls and Buffy the Vampire Slayer, with a whole wall dedicated to Britney Spears, Beyoncé and Madonna. I was especially obsessed with Madonna and what she represented to me. I couldn't put words to what she was doing, her sexual brazenness, her fearlessness, her politics, but what I did get was the sense of a woman who didn't give a fuck about the opinions that others had of her, and that felt good.

I wanted to reach out and have friends. I was sweetly naïve and had underestimated just how much loathing there was in a conformist society for the parts of me that were different. I decided I'd be the first person to throw a party for my class with a girl from my swimming team. I was attending an all-boys school so I thought if she invited her class and I invited mine, then the boys and the girls could get to meet each other. It seemed like a simple enough idea at the time. My parents hired out the town hall and I jumped at the opportunity to showcase my early fashionista instincts in an oversized silk shirt which was black on one side and white on the other, with gold buttons down one side. It had felt to me like something Michael or Janet

Jackson might wear, both of whom I was obsessed with at the time. Everyone came, the boys all wearing preppy polo shirts buttoned up to the chin, doused in their Dad's aftershave, standing huddled together looking sullen and nervous, unwilling to express any emotion apart from the absolute terror they felt at approaching the girls. The girls laughed and chatted among themselves and seemingly had a great time. I was perfectly comfortable to speak to them and so I had a great time too.

The next day at school, the boys told me that the party was shit, even the ones who didn't attend. I hadn't understood it at the time but processing the experience later, I could see that their internal narrative meant that they were scared of approaching girls at that age. Girls and femininity were of course seen as something to be dominated, conquered, something that might otherwise be a source of humiliation. They hadn't had the courage to talk to girls and they hated me for being able to do it and for putting them in a position that exposed their vulnerabilities to themselves. Worse still, they stood there watching the girls have fun without them. How dare they!? How they hated me for it. I went from feeling excited that I'd thrown the first party at high school, to feeling like I'd provided them with more ammo to hate me.

★

Adolescence is isolating enough and the unhappiness that I was experiencing was not intrinsically because of my identity. It was because I was attempting to fit into a precast mould of who society said I should be – male, straight and, ideally, white – and because of how, and who, other people assumed me to be. The root of my impending depression was a lie. I was led to believe that being Black, being queer and being feminine were bad things. I was expected to pretend that some identities simply didn't exist, even though they patently did.

In terms of diversity, inclusion and representation, I was growing up during an especially bland cultural moment. The mainstream appeared to offer one kind of beauty framed as the pinnacle to aspire to. If I wanted to be seen to be as attractive as my peers, that was the type of beauty I would somehow have to possess or at the very least emulate, so I'd already lost from the outset. It's easy to dismiss it now, having found a community that affirms every part of me, and having now been able to recognise the beauty in my own difference and the beauty in the difference of others. It's easy to forget while society is itself transitioning and dismantling some of these reductive ideas about beauty standards. Not that it's moving towards a place of perfection or true equality, but some differences can be spoken of with more ease, while we continue to demonise others. It is harder now to imagine the degree of isolation I felt in a society where there was no place for me, no one to reach out to or see myself reflected in. Without any evidence of diversity, it could be argued that such a thing didn't exist, that it wasn't necessary, that it didn't apply. But if you don't seek out reality and truth about the way the world is, all you're left with is ideology and indoctrination about how those in power want the world to be.

I couldn't tell you when I knew I was queer or when I knew I was trans; I didn't just wake up one day and have an epiphany. I think on a spiritual level I've always known. I had gone into puberty early – around the age of ten, actually – and I found it to be extremely distressing. I felt very self-conscious. I was still at primary school and became uncomfortable showing my legs and my armpits, embarrassed by the thick hair that had appeared suddenly, almost overnight. I broke out in acne on my forehead, which I was soon teased about. Because it was so visible, on the outside of me, I tried desperately to control it with anything and everything in my mother's medicine cabinet, but nothing seemed to work. Of course, I wasn't the only one experiencing changes in my body in these early stages of transitioning into adolescence, but there was something that felt particularly alien to me back then in seeing my body masculinise. While the kids around me seemed to be at ease, growing into themselves, I felt like I was losing myself, as if I couldn't recognise my reflection, as if I was wearing a disguise. As my muscle density increased and my body changed further, I would try to starve the masculinity out of myself. I couldn't skip dinner because we'd eat as a family, but I'd skip breakfast if I could, and lunch. I was happy to avoid eating in the lunch hall at school, as more often than not I didn't have anyone to sit with.

I made the decision to come out as gay when I was fourteen to two of the kids at school, Nathan and Joe. We didn't have much in common, but they also didn't have any friends apart from each other, so we formed an unspoken geeks' alliance of convenience at the back of the library, where none of the 'popular' kids could hurl abuse at us. I thought at the time that perhaps it would be easier for me if I just said it and 'owned up to it' as if it were a neighbour's window I'd accidentally broken. It felt like a good strategy for when the kids taunted me at school.

I'd briefly tried the other thing, emulating their version of masculinity. I tried to walk how they walked, I lowered my voice, I tried to change my interests and hobbies, but I kept hitting a wall. I couldn't deprogram myself. The idea of watching *Match of the Day* made me feel physically ill and running around playing rugby on a cold pitch just wasn't my idea of a good time. If they were going to come at me with homophobic slurs, then I thought coming out would neutralise them: 'Yeah, I am gay, so?' And in a sense, it worked, they were momentarily stumped, even though they continued to find other ways to be cruel. Transitioning into yourself is about recognising that it's never actually about the other person's view of you. If someone called me gay in a taunting manner today (without the threat of physical violence), I would think nothing of it because I am indeed queer as fuck and proudly so. But back then, even though I knew I was gay and even though I understood that being gay was not a thing to be shamed for, I was still ashamed. And that's the only reason it hurt, because a part of me believed in their slurs myself, and I couldn't see much else in the world around me that told me to think otherwise.

It took me another year to tell my mother. I finally told her one day after school when we were waiting for my brother to come out of the building. It was just her and me in a parked car in torrential rain. I'd played out the moment of me telling my mother in a thousand scenarios in my mind, pondering the perfect moment and environment that would soften the blow and minimise the fallout. But there didn't seem to be a particular time and place that felt ideal. So, I seized the moment. After all, here we were in a car alone, unable to go anywhere, with the rain beating down around us. I turned the radio off and asked my mum if she was proud of me. She said yes of course. I asked her if she'd always be proud of me and she didn't answer, knowing something was coming. I asked her if she'd be proud of me if I didn't *'like'* girls. It probably didn't come as a complete surprise, especially given certain internet searches I *may* have left on the family computer and certain hotlines I *may* have called on the landline. Let's just say I've never been very good at hiding anything. Yet still she took it pretty badly, to say the least.

Like many people at that time, my mother only knew queerness as tragedy. She had never seen any representation of queer joy. She immediately began to vocalise her concerns, what would life be like without a family, what would happen if I got sick. I wasn't even having sex at this point and instead of reassuring me, she trotted out a gruesome list of 'what ifs'. One of the reasons I'd wanted to tell her was to then be able to talk to her about the bullying that I was experiencing at school. Because if I couldn't tell her I was queer, I couldn't tell her why I was bullied. But it all went down so badly, I ended up not being able to tell her about the bullying anyway. We sat in silence till my brother got into the car and then we drove home, awkwardly listening to the sound of the rain and the swipe of the windscreen wipers for what felt like a teenage eternity.

My remaining time at home was characterised by froideur. I was immediately forbidden from telling my father. My mother was running with the classic 'it's just a phase'. 'Things will be different when you get older, when you get married and have children,' she'd tell me. In spite of this, I knew it was better to have everything out in the open as much as possible. Guilt and fear and negative feelings thrive in hidden spaces. This was a patch of sunlight to bathe in, even if there were a few patchy clouds above, killing the mood every now and again.

Teachers never stepped in at school when they heard homophobia being directed at me, though I had one favourite media teacher who covertly made it very clear that he wanted to. It turned out they weren't allowed to tell anyone off for being homophobic. I grew up during the years that Section 28, an amendment to the Local Government Act, was in effect. It had been passed as law in May 1988 under the then Prime Minister Margaret Thatcher's Conservative government. Section 28 declared that local authorities, which included schools, 'shall not intentionally promote homosexuality or publish material with the intention of promoting homosexuality' or 'promote the teaching in any maintained school of the acceptability of homosexuality as a pretended family relationship'. It was partly brought into force after a copy of a children's book, *Jenny Lives with Eric and Martin*, had been found in the library of a school run by a Labour Council.

This was a Danish book, translated into English, written for children who might, as the author pointed out, have come across family groupings that they weren't familiar with – and to assure the children who did live in these family settings that they existed and were perfectly normal, accessible and healthy arrangements. All its author wanted to do was to normalise alternative family structures – divorced families; single-parent families; families with two mothers; or families with two fathers. It had absolutely nothing to do with sex. But Thatcher and much of her government did not see it that way. 'Children,' declared the Prime Minister, 'who need to be taught traditional moral values are being taught that they have an inalienable right to be gay. All these children are being cheated of a sound start in life.' And so, I was cheated of my rights to support, to role models, to not feel as if my very existence was wrong. I accepted school in the way that one might accept prison – cordoned off from society with a bunch of men doing time together, counting down my six-year sentence, one rugby game and maths class at a time.

Academically, I lacked focus. However, despite this, I've always been extremely driven and focused on what I want for my future. I always knew fashion was what I wanted to be involved in, even though I didn't know how. I hid in the loos reading back issues of British *Vogue* and *Elle*. I spent a lot of my school life daydreaming, thinking about how everything I was learning didn't have anything to do with what I wanted to achieve. Whenever people would ask me what I wanted to do with my life, I never had a job in mind; I always gave big answers about wanting to be creative. I didn't want to fulfil a role or an expected purpose. I had no role models who'd done it before.

★

The experience of adolescence can be an extremely isolating one if the natural validation we seek can't be seen or heard in the world around us. Without being exposed to visible role models or role options, without a point of reference from someone we can relate to or see ourselves in, the world can be a difficult place to make sense of. It is possible to be what you cannot see, but it's ten times harder. Safety was a given for so many of my peers, but I found safety in those who allowed me to be myself, who didn't question what I naturally gravitated towards. Those adults who saw the unfiltered me and accepted me, who saw the real me, even a glimpse of the future me, and didn't try to stifle the spark – that is where I found my reassurance, my safety.

The shame and guilt that I developed during my adolescence are two emotions that as an adult I have worked especially hard to stamp out of my psyche. But on the rare occasion that the feelings creep in, I can almost sense myself being thrust backwards to how I felt after a day at school. The shame of being different and the guilt of not being good enough can become overwhelming. Role models show us that we are good enough as we are. They are a reminder that we don't need to reach for the unattainable and unrealistic expectations of who society says we should be. They challenge us to be the best version of ourselves in a fulfilling and sustainable way, that also uplifts and empowers those around us. During my adolescence, I needed to feel the approval of someone like me. I needed a role model, I needed to know that it was OK to be exactly who I was. But there was no one who shared the immediate intersections of my identity: queer, Black, transgender and of mixed heritage. It wasn't that these people didn't exist, but they were consciously hidden, socially censored out of public view and erased from history. There was no mainstream, easily accessible representation for someone like me to feel empowered by, and there wouldn't be for a long time to come.

You often don't realise that things are changing at the time when they are changing. Now pop culture is scrutinised and analysed immediately on social media, it's so much easier to form a new opinion. Back then there were no think pieces and no hot takes from the general public. You just had columnists back then, and even in the liberal media their ideas could be pretty conservative. They hadn't fully grasped the power of pop culture yet. But change was coming.

★

Two things happened when I reached sixth form: there were now gay people on the most mainstream of US TV shows; and our sixth form went co-ed. I needed this break, as even though the finishing line was in sight, being sixteen and seventeen was particularly difficult. It was one thing to imagine that school would end with escape from this town and this life, but it was another when you faced the pressure of that freedom being contingent on exams. It was also a time of sky-rocketing hormones, of my body changing into something that felt increasingly alien to me, and of school bullying becoming just ostracisation. I was invisible.

Being invisible didn't feel like much of an im provement on being an object of loathing; previously I was at least somehow included, even if it was to torment me. Now I was consciously ignored, treated like a ghost, barged into in the hallway as if I couldn't be seen. If they couldn't bully me then they would erase me.

Also, at sixteen, as far as the world outside school was concerned, I was now a Black male adult and the racism of my childhood felt entirely benign compared to the reactions I now inspired. Any kindness attached to me being a child was stripped away. My innocence was now gone in the eyes of society without my having done anything.

When girls joined the school, I finally made a friend. The TV shows *Will & Grace* and *Sex and the City* were two juggernauts at the forefront of a cultural shift that was making it seem cool for girls to have gay best friends. But this was often conditional, of course. The gay man was expected to be waspish, fabulous and funny, someone who would essentially act as a sidekick for the girl. The role of main character was off the table.

My friend Jemma was beautiful, outrageously so. She looked like a perfect porcelain doll, with long blonde hair and height that had her head and shoulders above most of her peers. She was working as a model already in commercials and fashion shows, alongside doing her AS levels. The boys fell all over her and so being friends with her afforded me some level of protection from them – at the very least, acknowledgement of my existence without being spat at.

Jemma and I discovered that we shared a common bond. The way that she was treated was often based on how she looked and not on who she was on the inside, just like me. Older men would leer at Jemma when she was still a child. The other girls thought she must deem herself better than everyone else, projecting their insecurities onto her in a similar way that the boys had projected their fears onto me. Teachers would see her beauty and talk to her as if she was stupid. She was sharp as a tack and went on to become a successful stockbroker and later an international businesswoman. It was an unspeakable relief to have someone to discuss my life with.

On my seventeenth birthday I got a car, which felt like an unutterable freedom. I passed my driving test, and now running away was replaced by driving to previously undiscovered places, music blasting and cigarette in a hand hanging out the window. Suddenly I didn't feel as isolated, as stuck, as I had for years. I'd drive to school and back every day, thankful that I no longer had to face the routine humiliation of being taunted on the coach. I had time and space to myself. Jemma and I took full advantage of our new getaway vehicle. We would go for lunch to the local Pizza Express on Fridays, really thinking that we were living our own *Sex and the City* moment. Her parents were wealthy and they lived in a large country house a few villages across from the school that you could only get to by car. So we would often spend free periods doing television work-outs together, chain-smoking menthol cigarettes at the bottom of her sizeable garden and swimming in her pool during the summer months.

My main focus, though, was still on getting away from home, as far as I could go, to Glasgow if they'd have me (which they wouldn't). I'd like to think I'd have done better academically if I hadn't been so thoroughly depressed for years, probably clinically depressed, albeit undiagnosed. Still, my three Bs at A level were enough for my second choice, Brighton. I'd always had an interest in fashion, starting with the notion that it was a safe space for me to express myself, but my main focus had been on learning how to get my thoughts and feelings down on paper and explore different ways of being creative. With that in mind, I'd applied to read English Language with Media and Communication.

I was aware that Brighton was known for having a sizeable LGBTQ scene. It sounded vibrant and cosmopolitan, basically everything Stansted Mountfitchet – a town in which I didn't even know anyone who'd got divorced – wasn't. I was ecstatic. Euphoric. When I packed to leave, I took absolutely everything I wanted to keep in life as if I was never going to go back. I was a queer kid going to the city! I wanted to leave behind this shell I had made to protect myself. On the night I left, I shaved my hair into a curly Mohawk. I was going to get to Brighton a new person, my environment would be different, my reality would be changed and I would be happy for ever. Only escape doesn't work like that. You can't run away from yourself. The destination will always be you. I only stopped running away when I made myself into the home I no longer wanted to run away from. I wish I had come to that realisation sooner.

Sex

In a world that prioritises heteronormative narratives, oftentimes joy, romance and happiness are reserved for straight people. Everyone else just gets sexual acts. Straight society at large often fails to think past the physicality of things. I didn't know any gay people growing up before I began looking for sexual partners, but worse, I barely knew any stories in which joy was a possibility for queer people. The idea of gay marriage was deemed absurd, with opinions such as that of the future British Prime Minister Boris Johnson, who compared gay marriage to bestiality in his 2001 book *Friends, Voters, Countrymen*: 'If gay marriage was OK – and I was uncertain on the issue – then I saw no reason in principle why a union should not be consecrated between three men, as well as two men, or indeed three men and a dog.'

The idea of being gay and having a family of your own was also demonised, with parallels being drawn between same-sex parents and child abusers by the mainstream media. Same-sex parents often became headline fodder for the tabloid press, which led to them being harassed and targeted with homophobic abuse.

The prevailing heterosexual narrative in all media was conditioning me not to have any expectations of romance, of companionship, of a family of my own. For straight people sex is allowed to be part of a relationship, to be a part of love, but the association of sex with queer people is still considered by many to be solely of hedonism, sex clubs and dungeons, carnal desires. This is why even well-intentioned people may say, 'I'd turn [gay] for your partner', as a compliment, as if the same-sex relationship is entirely contingent on sexual attraction. Visibility is much improved now for queer people but even today in the mainstream, when people think of queer love, they think about sex in the first instance.

Our sexuality is defined by our sexual feelings, thoughts, desires and ultimately who we find sexually attractive. But what society finds attractive is forever in flux, and therefore so is what we are expected or conditioned to find attractive. Throughout history society's sexual appetite has changed and expanded in a manner that has impacted on almost everything that we are exposed to on a daily basis. Regardless of our orientation, sexuality is entwined into our identities in an inescapable way. Society either validates or shames us into understanding our own sexuality: not just what gender we are attracted to, but what body shape, race, features, size, ability, behaviour society deems 'attractive' and 'acceptable' at large. The evolution of our sexuality as a society is a transition in itself, one that is ever-evolving.

For many of us, defining our sexuality with a label such as (and not limited to) straight, gay, bi, lesbian, pansexual or asexual, not only helps to describe how we feel to others, but it also helps to establish our social identity. When we understand our sexuality, we are able to access a sense of community, support, culture and validation. Especially in a society that centres the heterosexual or 'straight' sexuality as the expected norm, and has done so throughout much of western history. The way in which our sexuality impacts on how we see ourselves greatly differs depending on how society validates or stigmatises our sexual feelings. For instance, the way in which a patriarchal society sexualises lesbianism and sex between two women is not the same as how the same society views sex between two men. We can also see this in how society is much more likely to validate a woman's bisexuality or attraction to more than one gender identity than it is to validate the bisexuality of a man.

My sexuality has evolved alongside the evolution of my wider identity. It isn't fixed, at least not in the way that much of society expects it or encourages our sexualities to be. My sexuality is fluid. I find *people* attractive and that attraction isn't dependent on their gender identity or genitalia. Personally, I feel a closeness to the word 'queer'. I find power in how it has been reclaimed and reappropriated by LGBTQIA+ activists and queer theorists of the late 1980s and early 1990s. It's been taken from its historical roots in oppression and reintroduced to a new generation as an inclusive umbrella term, celebrating the seemingly endless spectrum of identities within our community. For me it just feels less restrictive than other terms; it feels free, it feels liberating. But that's the beauty of sexuality: it's as individual as we are; it's an aspect of self that is highly personal, largely invisible to others, but ours to choose how we express and define.

When I say that my sexuality has evolved, I don't necessarily mean that it has changed. I've always had these feelings, but I have grown to understand myself, understand society and become closer to existing within a body and mind that exist in harmony with each other. I've found that feelings and understandings of self have become unlocked along the way. 'Sexual fluidity' is the closest way that I can describe it, a removal of blockages, shame, trauma and expectation. I identified as gay before my transition because within that body, in that society, at that time, I didn't know that there was anything else other than straight or gay. My attraction to men was so overpowering and society was telling me that those feelings were so wrong. I assumed that I must have been male and I assumed that I must have been gay because I was assigned male at birth, because I'm in this body that everybody refers to as male and because I find men's bodies sexually attractive. But as my body began to adjust during my gender transition, so did the way that I viewed sex and my sexuality.

A fact that isn't made clear often enough is that sex is what you do and sexuality is what you feel. You can have a feeling without having performed an act. You can be a child and not sexually active and still be queer; you can be celibate and still be queer; you can be in a relationship with someone of the opposite sex and still be queer. You can have sex with someone of the same sex and not be gay, and you can have sex with the opposite sex and not be straight. The majority, in this case the alleged majority, has controlled society for hundreds of years by portraying any sexual difference as perversion to be held at bay. If heterosexuality is to be upheld as the norm, then homosexuality will be portrayed as a perverted sexual urge, reduced to an act, with the suggestion of paedophilia and other predatory behaviors often thrown into the mix.

I remember an incident in my childhood on a family holiday at a seaside town, when we crossed paths with a visibly gay man while heading towards the public toilets on the pier. My dad, brother and

I were warned not to go near him by someone exiting the building: 'Watch out, there's a poof in there,' signalling for my dad to keep an eye on us, lest he molest us. In my childhood being a gay man and being a sexual predator were synonymous. In this environment of fear, I was absolutely terrified that I'd become a monster if I pursued my sexual urges or at the very least that I would be seen as one. As you can't scare yourself out of being the person you are, society has created one other option, hating yourself. At thirty-six years old, I know far too many queer people who have killed themselves as a result of depression rooted in shame and isolation. Far too many people who've died from drug overdoses fuelled by feelings of constantly having to find an escape from reality. They've died in numbers disproportionate to the rest of the population. In 2022, research carried out by Youth Chances found that 52 per cent of British LGBT people reported that they had self-harmed, compared to 35 per cent of heterosexual people; and 44 per cent of LGBT people had experienced suicidal thoughts, compared to 26 per cent of non-trans heterosexual respondents. Stonewall UK also found that 13 per cent of LGBT youngsters aged eighteen to twenty-four had attempted to take their own lives during that year.

The traditionally conservative narrative would have you believe that it's because there's something inherently wrong with us as queer people, that the gay or the transness can simply be suppressed or prayed away. But what's wrong with us is that we're often struggling to reconcile how we have been made to feel in the face of a societal narrative that constantly denies our humanity and our right to a future filled with the same joy, romance, happiness, opportunity and respect as if we were born straight or cisgender.

★

It's 1999, I'm twelve years old and *Queer as Folk*, a British television drama following the lives of three gay men living in Manchester, has just aired on Channel 4. *Queer as Folk* was the first time I ever saw queerness be humanised, the first time I saw queerness presented as more than *just* sex. In it, queer people were living fulfilled lives. They had fun! They had their own way of communicating with others, their own chosen family dynamics. They had long-term and short-term relationships out in the open. They were proud to be queer. *Queer as Folk* was a sexual awakening of a different sort. Before it, I'd assumed that the experience of being queer was that people stayed in the closet for ever, perhaps marrying to keep up appearances, and having furtive same-sex encounters on the side. It had never occurred to me, having never seen any queer people in my town, having never been told anything at school about sexuality, having largely only found porn online as representative of the queer experience, that this life also came with the possibility of joy.

While it was a drama, *Queer as Folk* was to me the first time I'd ever seen an authentic representation of queer people, as real people with layers, not just two-dimensional stereotypes or hypersexual deviants and deplorables. I'd watch it at night after my parents had gone to bed on the TV in my room. My parents made me leave my bedroom door ajar, so I'd memorised where the floor creaked and crept across the room to turn it on, watching it with the volume turned low. I felt like I'd been teleported into the real world, out of this level of purgatory, where I'd been lied to. I'd found a place where I didn't have to live in secrecy and isolation – a world where I'd always be able to be me. It became part of my grand fantasy of escape from Stansted Mountfitchet. It was also the first time I got an inkling of how to find my way into my real self, by actively seeking out the truth and thus being able to reject a bogus narrative of expected norms. But there were years yet before I got there.

*

A few months after coming out to my mum, I lost my virginity to a man I met on an internet chat room. He wasn't the first person I had spoken to, nor the first I had engaged in sexual activities with, but my limited understanding of what sex was meant that penetration equalled 'real sex', and this would be my first time doing so. I'd been using internet chat rooms to explore my sexuality, in a sense to find myself rather than other people. I'd chatted with a lot of people and generally selected people who were older than me because I wanted to engage with people with experience. Sometimes I'd pretend to be older but I'd told this man my real age. Before sixth form I didn't have any friends who I could trust to tell where I was going, who I was meeting or why I was meeting them, and I certainly couldn't have told my parents. I had no idea just how dangerous that situation could have become.

No adult should ever take advantage of an under-age teenager in an internet chat room, no matter what they may say, no matter how empowered they may, as a fifteen-year-old, claim to feel. We'd been speaking for a few days, but before even logging in, I'd already come to the decision that today would be the day that I was going to have 'full sex' for the first time. I hadn't given much thought as to who it would be with, as in my mind this was purely about me, my desires, my sexual frustrations and unanswered questions. I wanted to know how it felt to be intimate with another person. I wanted somewhere to put my feelings, to help me make sense of them. As I couldn't speak to people about my sexuality, I felt like this was the only way I could inhabit this part of myself.

He was in his mid-thirties. He didn't look like his pictures, to the extent that I didn't even think it was the same person standing in front of me, but by the time I'd taken a train to the next town and met him in the car park behind the station, I felt obliged to go through with it. I had built this moment up in my head to such a degree that who he was almost ceased to matter. Even so, it was a shambolic introduction to intimacy.

After an awkward drive to an unkempt house he shared with three other people, we headed directly to his room on the first floor. The sex was dismal. Even though the only thing I had to compare it to was the porn I'd surreptitiously consumed on our computer at home with the jarringly loud dial-up internet, I knew this wasn't how it was meant to be. There was no spark, no connection of any sort. Perhaps worst of all was the disarray of the room itself, where he had to make space for us between piles of crumpled clothes and empty crisp packets. I was horrified and repelled, but in that moment, in that room, after an hour-long drive from a way-out station, I didn't think I had the option of telling a man almost twenty years older than me that I'd 'changed my mind'. As he drove me back to the station, there was an uneasy silence, a different tension from the journey earlier that day, and when he parked, he leaned towards me. 'Let's keep this between us, yeah?' he said. I knew exactly what he meant and it creeped me out that he had waited until the last moment to acknowledge that what he'd done was wrong. Needless to say, we never saw each other again. This encounter was followed by a long series of hook-ups that followed a pattern of hopeful anticipation followed by swift and conclusive disappointment.

I was sixteen when I first felt that I'd made a real connection with someone. He was much older than me and a policeman. He was the first man I felt comfortable having sex with, whom I developed a connection with. He made me feel not only desirable, but also comfortable about being sexual with somebody. I began to enjoy sex in a way that it became less about the release and more about the experience.

But it wasn't without its dangers and pretty soon the new-found comfort and confidence he helped me build was exploited. The more comfortable he made me feel, the more he would encourage and coerce me into doing things that were not only illegal, but also put my health and mental well-being at risk. The balance of power was far from equal in our relationship. I hadn't the experience or sexual education to understand the wider implications of being encouraged to engage in sexual acts that could have had serious consequences.

After a couple of months of hooking up with him I was feeling pretty confident in myself and open to trying new things in bed. In the moment I felt empowered, sexy and in control of the situation. One day he talked me into letting him fuck me without a condom and film it with a camcorder. The idea of making a sex tape didn't particularly turn me on, but I could see it was clearly turning him on and that made me want to go through with it. He told me that sex 'feels so much better without a condom', that 'everybody does it', and when I raised concerns about sexually transmitted infections, he insisted that he had 'just been checked'.

Of course, now I know he was grooming me and I was being exploited by a person in a position of power and trust. While I was legally of age to have sex − just − I was absolutely not old enough to consent to be filmed having sex, even if it was just for his own viewing. He had managed to coerce me into participating in underage pornography and taken advantage of the fact that I was woefully uneducated about the importance of safe sex. I did, of course, know vaguely what HIV was, but because no one had ever talked to me about it, any sort of danger felt unreal, far away, something that couldn't possibly happen to me.

★

The more sex I had with strangers, the more sex became a secret release in my teens, a way to feel less alone and more validated within my sexuality. Even though

I didn't actually enjoy it, I craved it. I hadn't yet figured out that sex for sex's sake wasn't really my vibe and that connection is paramount, it's the key that unlocks genuine pleasure. Pleasure that goes way beyond and way deeper than a stranger touching, kissing or fucking me. As I well know now, genuine intimacy and sex do not necessarily come hand in hand. But back then, it was enough to be seen as desirable; that is what brought speed to my blood, what kept me going back for more. In the absence of the validation of my sexuality in any other part of my life, this was critical to my sense of well-being. It wasn't just the physical. It was also, even if subconsciously, an overwhelming need to understand my place in the world, to understand why I was feeling what I was feeling.

Even though I had found some solace in hooking up with men who were able to accept me for who I was, little of it was straightforward and much of it was fraught and confusing. Sex with strangers, sex with older men comes with risks and inevitably left me vulnerable to being exploited. I often lied about my age online, as I looked older than I actually was, though eventually, I figured out that being honest about how old I was attracted older men who wanted to have sex with me because I was so young. Like many young people curious about sex, I didn't see myself as a child. I didn't understand, let alone want to address, the dangers I was putting myself in.

None of this would have happened if I'd had a proper sex education, instead of being filled to the brim with shame by the world around me and forced to navigate my sexual awakening through a lens of porn and predatory men. My rush of optimism on seeing *Queer as Folk* had long dissipated, crushed by a lack of representation, of role models, of community. I couldn't understand how anyone could be proud to be gay. I carried that internalised shame consciously, forever on high alert that if I 'gave myself away' it could result in me being physically or verbally attacked. I used to feel like these hook-ups were a safe haven from the judgement that I would be exposed to every single day. But now I can see that I had just been pushed from one harmful environment into another.

With the right teaching, guidance, compassion and empathy – even a dusting of understanding – I could have understood more about sex itself. I often think about how I would have navigated those times much more easily if the teachers who wanted to support a student struggling with sexuality were legally allowed to. The way we transition from being unaware of our sexuality, to being aware of it and an active participant in it, is crucial for our development and how we grow into considerate, respectful and accepting adults. In my view, the way we talk about sex matters, and the way we *don't* talk about sex matters.

Like most people my age and older, my high-school sex-ed was woefully next to non-existent and exclusively focused on heterosexuality. I have a hazy memory of a supply teacher nervously putting a condom on a banana, and later, watching an unexpectedly graphic childbirth video, which prompted a few of my classmates to faint and fall off their science-lab stools. When the curriculum required teachers to talk about sex, it was always in the context of the heterosexual 'norm' and spoken about in a clinical manner devoid of pleasure, and queer or not, this approach didn't even begin to prepare me for my own future sexual encounters or help me to process my feelings.

Before I came out as gay, like most teenagers in the age of the internet, with uncontrollable hormones and a wandering mind, I'd turned to pornography, the only real option available to me. Now, let me be clear, I'm not anti-porn. But I am most definitely against porn being the only option available for young people to learn how to have sex. No thirteen-year-old should have to learn about sexual pleasure, future relationships and their own body by watching grown adults perform the act of sex, largely through the cisgender straight male lens.

Not talking about sex to young people doesn't mean that it won't happen or that they won't seek out other means of attempting to understand it. It just means that they will be woefully unprepared for what, like me, they'll most likely end up doing anyway. And when we fail to afford children a fair sex education because their identity isn't in keeping with what are considered 'traditional values', it sends a message about the perceived value of their future.

As I said earlier, homosexuality – let alone any other iteration of queerness – by law wasn't even allowed to be mentioned in any class, in any way, in school. Long story short: I had to keep myself hidden while also being a visible target. I wasn't able to voice who I was, I wasn't able to ask my teachers for any help in understanding my sexual identity because they weren't legally allowed to give it.

I felt trapped within myself, ashamed of who I was and isolated from the world around me. There is no doubt that for me, coming out was the beginning of transitioning out of shame; a release and realisation that the shame of others and my own shame could no longer cage me in and hold me back from becoming the best authentic version of who I was or who I could become, a version of myself that I could be proud of. I didn't know there was anything else other than straight or gay. I didn't have the reach or understanding or language beyond being gay. I'd been assigned male at birth; I was in this body that everybody referred to as male and my attraction to men was so overpowering. Transitioning out of shame and into pride is a process that involves us all, but it's also an experience that I and many other LGBTQIA+ people experience regularly. The idea that a queer person comes out once is a myth; we as queer people will find ourselves having to come out countless times over our lifetime, as the spaces that we frequent or people around us change.

In an ideal world, nobody should have to come out. But unfortunately, we don't live in an ideal world, and sexual stigma, shame, prejudice, bias, disinformation, discrimination, and still in some places criminalisation, all very much still exist across the planet, creating a culture of thinking that places queer sexual identity outside the norm. Who we are personally attracted to is a publicly defining aspect of our identity; we each have our own personal timeline for processing this part of the self.

Let's think critically about what the action of coming out or expecting an LGBTQIA+ person to come out, truly is. As a top line, coming out is ultimately disclosing the fact that you are not heterosexual/straight/cisgender. Which means that you arc disclosing that you find members of the same gender or multiple genders sexually attractive, or if you are trans, that you don't identify as the gender that you were assigned at birth. It's important to acknowledge that the coming-out conversation very rarely ends there; it creates an expectation for the person coming out to speak about their sex life, sexual desires and/or relationship status in a way that heterosexual people are simply not pressured into in the same way. Speaking about sex and relationships itself isn't the issue, but the fact that LGBTQIA+ people are expected to disclose details of their sexual identity when heterosexual people are not, *is* an issue. In expecting LGBTQIA+ people to come out, society not only 'others' queer people's feelings, but it also puts a pressure on those people to disclose their feelings before they are ready, before they are safe, supported, or before they are even certain of them themselves. When we take into consideration that the rates of young people identifying as exclusively heterosexual are falling, with just 66 per cent of Generation Z identifying as exclusively heterosexual or straight, we can safely say that queerness is rapidly becoming less and less of the social anomaly that previous generations believed and promoted it to be.

But it's not all negative. A by-product of LGBTQIA+ people being expected to be transparent and open with our sexual identity to a heightened degree is that we become more sexually liberated than our heterosexual counterparts. We are simply more used to speaking about sex and navigating uncomfortable conversations about how others view our sexual identity. By definition, the existence of LGBTQIA+ PRIDE is a defiance of heteronormative society's efforts to shame us as a community because of our sexual identities and desires.

If young people are identifying as LGBTQIA+ sooner and in higher numbers than ever before, that will also mean that they will be expected to speak about their sexual identity sooner and more widely. If we hope to level out the playing field, we need to ensure that we are starting conversations about all kinds of sexual feelings before that happens, so that all young people feel validated and seen within their sexuality rather than ashamed and hidden. All environments must uncentre heterosexuality as the norm and expected standard. We need to be inclusive, mindful and supportive of all identities from an early age. This is crucial if we hope to create an environment where coming out is no longer expected or necessary because we understand each other, because we value difference rather than seeing it as something that warrants disclosure. Transitioning out of sexual shame involves us all.

★

It's September 2005, and I'm leaving Stansted for university, driving down to Brighton with my parents and my brother. I have my headphones on for most of the journey to avoid dealing with my mum being upset and my dad not saying anything at all and me feeling hurt by it. Whatever either of them could have said wasn't what I needed. I wanted my dad to take an interest in me and my mum to stand up for me, for my parents to support me as I was rather than who I was expected to be. But as this wasn't going to happen, at least not yet, it is a headphones-on situation, a looking out of the window and pretending to be in a music video moment.

We get further and further away from all the landmarks that had defined my life up to this point. The shop where I used to work for pocket money, the bus stop that I'd wait at every morning before school, the gate to the nature reserve where I'd run to after arguing with my dad. The feeling of letting them go is liberating, empowering, cathartic. Driving past them feels like they no longer define me, that Stansted no longer has a hold on me, that with this new start I can be anyone or anything I want. As we arrive in Brighton I can't stop grinning with excitement, licking my lips to try and stop myself from smiling uncontrollably. Each unfamiliar, exciting landmark we drive past ignites the realisation that a reinvention of self is imminent, and life will finally be on my terms.

Once we reach my new home, my parents help me offload my boxes from the car and carry them up the stairs to my new room. Prior to moving to Brighton, I had visited the city with my mum to try and find accommodation for the first year of my studies. My course was based on Falmer campus, located a half-hour bus journey from the city centre, in the middle of what seemed like an endless expanse of fields. As soon as we got there, I knew that it wasn't going to work for me; I didn't even need to see the halls of residence to make a decision. The seclusion of it felt like Stansted, a world away from the picture of freedom that I had envisioned for my big escape. I attended a networking event for students who wanted to seek out private accommodation house-shares with other first years, where I hit it off with four other students who were also interested in finding a house as close to the city centre as possible. My housemates-to-be were all straight, three girls and a guy. We were all studying different courses on different campuses and I could tell that we didn't have masses in common, but they seemed nice enough and my real priority was the location.

We ended up finding a property in Kemptown, Brighton's gay village, walking distance from the seafront and all the gay bars that I was so desperate to hit up. Some of the rooms were bigger than others, so we drew straws over a getting-to-know-you drink, for who got which space. I struck lucky with a big bedroom at the top of the house. Things were finally looking up.

After my parents drop my belongings off, we have some sandwiches and tea before they set off back home to Stansted. I'm pretty quiet and at this point, frankly I'm just waiting for them to leave so I can get down to the business of living. My mum gives me a hug, and I realise how much I'm going to miss her. A pang of guilt flips my stomach upon realising how happy I am feeling about escaping, when she has sacrificed and provided so much for me. But then I realise that it's not her that I'm running away from. I am running away from everything, and it's beyond anything that I could possibly put into words at that point, including myself and the truth of who I am. My dad gives me an awkward man-hug and pats me on the back: 'Look after yourself, stay safe,' he says, as they make their way to the car. As I wave them off from the doorway of my new home, an overwhelming sense of freedom hits me. This is it; this is the start.

I step back inside the house, closing the door behind me. I run up the stairs to my room and unpack a box that I had marked with a thick black X in permanent felt-tip. Inside it are all of the trinkets that I had collected in secret and hidden over my final years in Stansted, ready for my new life: make-up, perfume, magazines and clothing that I had been keeping in a locked box at the back of my old wardrobe. Lip gloss given to me by Jemma, shoplifted fragrances too sweet to wear without raising an eyebrow, copies of *Attitude* magazine and nail polish that came free with fashion titles. I pull out a customised pair of jeans and a grey faux fur jacket and put them on, then dab on some purple-tinted berry lip balm and creamy bronze metallic eyeshadow, and stand back to look at myself in the mirror. I see potential, I feel an unfamiliar sense of freedom in the person looking back at me. A smile of relief spreads across my face. I am going to meet my people. People who I can see myself in and will see me for me.

For the first few months of our first semester, I spent most my free time hanging with the girls of the house, Jade, Sariah and Kim. Paul, the boy who we shared with, was older than us and in a long-term and long-distance relationship, so usually kept himself to himself. Having never lived with anyone other than our families before, we were all starting to pick up on each others' varying levels of home comforts, tidiness, bad habits and personality quirks. We all did things that annoyed the others, small things, unintentional things that would build up into big irritations. Jade had a tendency to have extremely loud sex that kept the whole house up all night, every other night. Sariah was unpredictable, with a different mood and different drama for each day of the week. Kim loved to bitch about everyone in the house, but when confronted about it denied absolutely everything. I, on the other hand, definitely wasn't the most enthusiastic when it came to cleaning and certainly wasn't that great at it. What started off as a concerted effort to form sisterly friendships after a few months quickly turned into strictly housemate territory. Which I wasn't that bothered by, except when it came to time to collect everyone's money for the monthly bills, which was my responsibility and often the only interaction that I had with some of them.

Like a lot of first-year students at university who had moved from a small town to a city, I spent my weekdays partying all night and trying not to fall asleep in lecture theatres. My social battery at full capacity, I had no problem going to bars and clubs on my own. I had found a sense of community on the queer scene, but it just wasn't exactly how I thought it would be. I met a lot of people my own age who, like me, had been quite isolated in their sexuality, who weren't yet able to express their feelings and their fears. Everyone was having a lot of firsts: first big romances, first heartbreaks, first big sexual experiences. People were finding out what scene they wanted to be part of. I remember one of my friends was beginning to experience BDSM and figuring out what part of queer culture they fitted into – a bear, a twink, an otter? I wasn't sure where I fitted in. I'd often find myself being referred to as a 'fem' or a 'tranny', depending on who was describing me. All the boys who fell outside the confines of traditional masculinity were often identified as such. Being referred to as fem didn't really bother me because I was feminine, I liked my femininity and I loved that I had arrived at a place where I wasn't the only one. But to be called a 'tranny', even if in jest, felt confronting and commodifying. It felt like my femininity was mocked, degraded, as if I was somehow there for the entertainment or the pity of others. I couldn't put my finger on why it bothered me so much at the time, but it did, that much I knew.

I'd found a community of other people who were also running away from trauma, running away from loneliness, trying to escape their hurt. I'd found gay men terrified of femininity, especially their own. I was, once again, too feminine. Everyone wanted to be with a guy who could pass as straight; everyone was so wounded by their own experience that they had internalised society's homophobia and made it into a part of themselves. Having been taunted as not 'real' or 'proper' men in a patriarchal culture, they felt masculinity was something to seek out as a trophy.

Brighton was also whiter than I'd expected, and definitely more uncritically white. Being Black in a very white scene meant that it was rare to be seen as sexy without being fetishised. I'd been exposed to racism in Stansted but there was a brashness and often a sexualised nature about it in Brighton. It was as if people thought that being LGBTQ negated the possibility of being racist, that one didn't have to worry about racism because we were all queer. Naively and perhaps with a sprinkle of the narcissism of young adulthood, I was expecting a flurry of sexual interest in me, but it didn't materialise. I'd gone from having no access, to feeling like I was going to have access but ending up as a spectator – again. Anytime I was found attractive, people would be astonished, and worse still, it happened so infrequently that I found myself being astonished too. Other queer people would say outright, 'I don't sleep with Black people.' So many Black people had been conditioned to see whiteness as the beauty standard to aspire to. I could even see that behaviour in myself, in how I would scan a club, how I would google porn. I'd not do it deliberately, but I could see where my attention would go, what kind of person I would find attractive, who I would romanticise.

Even today, I grapple with the shadows of unlearned indoctrination, even today. I know we all like what we like and who we like, but when it comes down to the specifics of why we find someone attractive, who we prioritise romantically (not just sexually) and what we think beauty is, so much of it comes down to where we were raised and who we were told is beautiful from an early age. I have had to consciously unpack and uproot these ideas, actively working to decolonise my understanding of sex, love and beauty. A lot of those negative ideas of self-hatred, of not finding Blackness attractive, even if unconsciously, were held because I'd been told that I and other Black people were not attractive for as far back as I can remember. The voices, views and downright lies of others had been internalised.

In my first term, I didn't have anything resembling a romantic relationship, and continued in my old familiar patterns. I would meet older men – never other students – and have largely anonymous sex. Being in the city didn't change the outcome so much, though it did change some of my methods. I wouldn't just meet men online, I'd meet them on nights out, I'd meet them in smoking areas outside clubs, I'd even meet them on the street walking home at night. I was used to the dynamic of older men. It required me to be submissive and I was at home with that; it was all I knew.

One of the men I struck up a connection with was a drag performer in town. His humour and charm were apparently reserved for the stage. I was there to be fucked, not to be known or held; I was just a body to him. Unexpectedly he handed me an envelope with an emotionless, uncaring facial expression after we had sex for the first time, asking me not to question him or open it until he had left. It contained £100 in worse-for-wear bank notes. I'm not entirely sure what his reasoning was, but I'm pretty sure it was hush money to make sure that I didn't say anything. It would also mean that if I were to out him for sleeping with me, I would also out myself as the sex worker that I apparently now was. Or perhaps it was to make sure that I came back for more: more money, if not more sex? Being unexpectedly handed £100, as a broke nineteen-year-old university student, for sex that I had already engaged in, didn't feel like the manipulation that I can now see it was, but I guess that was the point.

I was beginning to understand that without connection sex felt empty. That's what I was truly seeking, what I truly wanted. True connection.

Gender

I'm often asked, 'So when did you first realise you were transgender?' But there was no eureka moment, no instantly recognisable moment of awakening. I knew I didn't feel right in my body when I hit puberty and whatever changes I was making in my life were happening blindly and organically. When people come to realise that they're trans, there's sometimes a defining point. But usually, it's a long series of clues that all add up to point in the same direction. I just gravitated towards what I felt close to and where I felt freedom.

Modern western society is heavily rooted in binary gendered coding, from pink for girls to blue for boys, from Barbie to Action Man, and from skirts to trousers. Until very recently gender roles have been clearly defined and socially upheld, especially in the media, often placing men as the heroes and women as the damsels in need of being rescued. Men are often framed as the protagonist, while women adopt the role of sidekick or love interest. Men are believed to be logical decision-makers, while women are seen as the emotional counsel. The Hollywood model of the nuclear family consisting of a husband and wife with two kids is often still considered the goal.

Along with gender stereotypes, we're all brainwashed from an early age into believing that the gender binary is real. There has been little western acknowledgement of the identities that lie between and outside this concept on a global scale. Why do we subscribe to such binary assumptions of who children and adolescents are, based on the gender that they are assigned at birth? Are we unconsciously participating in an archaic form of colonial indoctrination, rather than encouraging young people to figure out who they are organically? Currently our gender identity is decided for us by the state, depending on whether we are born with a penis, a vagina or both. Even if our parents wanted to say, 'I'd rather my child decided what gender they wish to be,' gender is still registered by the state depending on our genitals. We are robbed of the chance to recognise ourselves outside of our state-sanctioned identity. But we are individuals, our perceptions of gender are based on our experiences, and those are unique to us.

Transgender-exclusionary radical feminists, or TERFs, seem to fear liberation for everyone, as if a trans woman being treated like a human being somehow negates their own sense of oppression as women. In some ways TERFs highlight the real problem; they are right to feel threatened by men, but trans women aren't men and are under the same assault from patriarchy and the way masculinity functions in society as any other woman. All women are liberated by revolutionising the systems we live in. So many TERFs want to maintain a system that has hampered both their and my ability to be present in the world.

Four months after the big move, I had fully immersed myself in the hedonism of Brighton's queer culture. I'd met a fun group of people during a vodka-soda-fuelled Fresher's bar-crawl – four gay guys and a lesbian. We quickly hit it off, regularly meeting up for nights out, Sunday roasts, days at the beach and trips to the cinema. Although I had absolutely no experience in hospitality, I'd managed to blag my way into a job at a popular gay venue on the seafront. I thought it would be a good way to meet people and expand my social life.

It was a new and exciting feeling to not have to water myself down, even though at times I still found myself doing so as force of habit. I was beginning to feel freer within my gender expression, dressing the way I wanted and not censoring my mannerisms. My personal style had started to evolve. I grew my hair out like I had always wanted to, spraying it into a tall mohawk that I amped up at night with weft extensions. I started experimenting with make-up and nail art, with acrylics when I could afford them. I reshaped my eyebrows with a more feminine arch and started wearing women's tops and jeans, sometimes with a pair of heels when I was feeling brave. I had adopted the gender-neutral nickname 'Munroe', given to me by one of my new friends as there was another person in our group with the same birth name as me. He thought of it after noting the piercing that I had on the left side of my upper lip, which is known as 'the Monroe', as it mimics Marilyn's mole. The name stuck. I was silently relieved and excited. My birth name had come to remind me of school and bullying. This new name felt like a welcome slice of freedom, a shot at a do-over.

I'd go home occasionally, short sporadic trips no longer than a weekend. Heading back to Stansted felt like going back in time, regressing into my old self. It felt like nothing had changed at home. But I most definitely had. Usually, I would turn up in a bit of make-up, a girl's top and painted nails. It wasn't my full look but it felt closer to who I was than I had ever been in Stansted before. I guess it felt like a bit of a 'fuck you', a quiet rebellion, affirming that I was an adult now and not living under my parents' roof any longer.

Mum was highly critical of how I presented myself. 'Can't you be more boyish?' she'd say, 'those eyebrows are a little thin,' and 'Do you have to have your nails that long?' Dad wouldn't say anything at all, but I could see him looking at my nails in disapproval out of the corner of his eye. The atmosphere was strained to say the least, but when had it not been?

Summer break had arrived and the last thing I wanted to do was spend it twiddling my thumbs in Essex, so I got a job on the door of a drag club instead. I found drag euphoric. Before I had the language to be able to identify as trans, I would refer to myself as a queen. Drag unlocked part of myself that I'd never experienced before. It was more than just make-up, a wig, heels and a tight dress. It was the feeling of waking up, of accessing the confidence to be fully present, fearless and bold. Going out in drag made me feel like the best version of myself; I felt liberated, as if I was able to wear my feelings for everyone to see, without shame, without filter.

With the meteoric rise of shows such as *RuPaul's Drag Race* now gaining deserved success in the mainstream, drag has gained more social acceptance than it once had. Concurrently, in the eyes of heteronormative society it's also become seen as less radical, less confronting, as if it's just another reason to dress up. But at its heart, drag is revolutionary. Drag forces you to confront everything about yourself, about your identity. It urges you to unpack your relationship with gender and who you present yourself as. Everything we wear is a reflection of how we see ourselves and how we want the world to see us. We're performing ourselves, different drag for different environments and different moods. When you really boil it down, everything we do is drag, everything we put on our bodies is drag, all our self-expression is a performance of gender. It raises the question of what gender is other than a performance. Our most organic self is us naked, bare; everything else, really, is just a form of drag.

I referred to my gender expression as 'drag' at the time because I guess that's what it was, but in tandem it was a way for me to explore my true gender identity and access a feeling of affirmation that I had long been searching for, but hadn't yet been able to pinpoint or vocalise. Drag helped me to combat my anxiety and social awkwardness. It brought a joy to my life that allowed me to feel at home in my body. It changed how I saw myself. I went from being largely mirror-evasive to feeling affirmed, empowered, almost as if I had seen myself for the first time. It gave me the confidence to do uncomfortable things, like eventually calling my father to talk to him about my love life and my sexuality — something I had long been avoiding. His response was masked disappointment and awkwardness, but I felt the relief of laying claim to myself again, of not hiding parts of my life as if they were too shameful to mention. I felt that perhaps by finally acknowledging the elephant that had always been in the room, we could lay a foundation to build some kind of relationship that felt better than the one we already had.

The crash after this great big summer high followed in my second year in Brighton. I was out all night, every night, crawling to lectures the next day after a sit-down shower and a strong cup of coffee, usually sleeping on the bus on my way to campus. At first it felt manageable, exciting even, this terrifically full life. But after my first year I was starting to miss deadlines, even though I loved my course and had always felt passionately about writing. I'd stopped visiting my parents altogether, and at one point I also stopped calling them or returning their calls. On some days I was exhausted, depleted and wanted nothing other than to lie down and close the curtains, sleep the day away and hope that tomorrow would feel less heavy. This went on until some days started to become most days, and then most days became every day. I booked an appointment with my local GP to see if they could help. I thought I was just stressed and overwhelmed with university work; mental health wasn't such an open conversation at this point. I remember sitting down in the GP's office and not being able to look her in the eye, as I could see that she was visibly concerned at what she saw. She asked if she could weigh me and whether I had noticed any disruption to my appetite or eating habits.

For years I had managed to keep the secret of limiting my food intake as a method of control, but now I felt like I was finally being busted. I denied any suggestion that I was experiencing an eating disorder, in the same way I'd always denied it. With my sunken cheeks, glazed expression and ribs protruding in my chest and back, I could tell that she wasn't buying any of it. As the appointment dragged on, it felt harder and harder to say 'I'm OK' or 'I'm fine'; I couldn't even convince myself any more. I sat down as I tried to force a smile that wouldn't come, then to my surprise I started crying. I cried and shook hysterically, doubled over in my seat. She got up from behind her desk and hugged me until I stopped, then told me that she believed I was showing signs of anorexia, severe anxiety and depression. She prescribed me a combination of pills that I started taking that afternoon, but warned me that it might take a little time to feel better or find the medication that was the right match for me. I left the surgery unsure of how I should feel. I was happy to have some answers, yet terrified of the road to recovery ahead, and I didn't know if I truly had the will to fight for it.

After a month and a bit, I could feel that the pills were starting to have an effect on my mood and outlook. I felt different, lighter almost. I found myself able to get more university work done as it was easier to get out of bed for lectures in the mornings, easier to focus and absorb information. My appetite also improved, but I couldn't tell if it was the shock of being told that I was anorexic and dangerously underweight, or whether I actually wanted to eat. I knew I didn't want to die, so I assumed that it must be a combination of both. For a while everything seemed fine again; it was insufficient, but it was something. I'd put a Band-Aid on a broken leg. The truth is, I'd been looking for anything that would help me break out of my reality, and chasing euphoria more than joy in Brighton. The euphoria of getting out, of enjoying my appearance, of doing what I wanted. Joy is sustainable; euphoria is not. You can be massively unhappy and still induce euphoria.

*

Pushing my diagnosis to the back of my mind, I unexpectedly spent the summer break after my second year back in Stansted. My parents were under a lot of stress that year – illness in the family, along with other things – so I decided not to tell my mum about being diagnosed with anorexia, depression and anxiety. I didn't want to worry her and add to an already very full plate. I could tell it was all getting a bit much for her; she looked tired and drawn. She could tell that I wasn't OK, but I always brushed it off. The truth that I had an eating disorder was not one that I was fully ready to accept. Although it was massively unhealthy for both my body and my mind, it made me feel like I had something I could control, even though it was clearly controlling me.

With the few friends that I had made in sixth form having now moved away, I hopped online to try and make some queer friends and stem the familiar pangs of isolation that were creeping back in. I was spending a lot of time alone again, visiting the places I found solace in as a teen. My parents had sold my car when I left for university, so getting around took planning. I missed the freedom of having easy access to a community, being able to joke around with people I had things in common with. I missed being the uncensored and carefree self that I had started to explore and embrace before I got ill. Stansted was pretty bare when it came to finding LGBTQ friends my own age; most were either still in the closet and just wanted to hook up, or they were older, in a relationship and looking for a third. The SSRIs had well and truly fucked up my sex drive, so neither option much appealed. I needed and craved the unique intimacy of queer friendship.

Shane worked at the airport about thirty minutes from my house. We had got chatting on a website called Facepic and after getting to know each other, decided to meet up for a bottle of wine after one of his shifts. I hadn't laughed so much in ages. We had the same stupid dark sense of humour and disdain for the strait-laced slow pace that our corner of Essex had to offer.

I played it cool but I had a bit of a crush on him. I wasn't sure if it was genuinely romantic or whether it was just misconstrued feelings of relief that finally, I had found someone to talk to, someone I could hug, giggle with and vent to, someone I could vent *with*, someone who understood what it was like to grow up queer and isolated in a place like this.

A couple of months into the summer break, I was getting ready to meet Shane for some drinks at a pub garden a few towns over. I asked my parents if he could come over afterwards to watch some movies, order a takeaway and then stay the night. Needless to say, my Dad refused. But living in Brighton had changed me, and I no longer saw my dad as the hypermasculine authority figure of my youth. So I challenged him, which led to a big fight. I felt like he couldn't accept who I was, and pushing back felt like what I had to do in order to avoid returning to the mindset of my adolescence. It didn't end well. I packed my bags and headed back to the Brighton that day.

Being back in Brighton was tough, as I really didn't know what to do with myself or how to feel. My mental health wasn't getting any better, and the fight with my family weighed heavily on my mind. My twenty-first birthday rolled around at the end of the summer and Mum came to visit. I wasn't expecting

Dad to join her, yet still found myself surprised by the disappointment I felt that he didn't show up to see me on such a milestone birthday. Everyone in my family is stubborn, including me, but I guess part of me hoped that maybe (if only for a day) we could put our feelings on one side and be a family.

A bright spot in this difficult time was meeting a new friend called Demi. We met at a house party after a night out on the seafront. She was like nobody I had ever met before. Demi was a glamazon, one of those stunningly beautiful people you'll walk past in the street and for a split second forget your own name. She was next-level gorgeous. I remember seeing her in silhouette, standing by the window with a cigarette, not a hair out of place, serenely watching the sun come up. She offered a stark contrast to a room full of partied gays in jockstraps running on the fumes of a three-day drug binge. I felt drawn to her, as if I was supposed to know her or at least talk to her. I had no idea that she was transgender until somebody outed her to me in the kitchen while shoving a generous bump of ketamine up their nose. 'Can you believe that's a tranny,' they crassly said in enamoured disbelief. I couldn't get over how beautiful she was and, after speaking to her, how… 'normal' she was. By just being there and talking to me about how she had ended up in Brighton, she debunked and transcended everything negative that I had internalised about being trans. Without knowing it, she gave me permission to be excited about accessing a part of myself that had always existed behind a closed door. A door that I had always been too afraid to open. I could tell that she could see the real me and I knew that she knew that I knew...

Although she was still young, it felt like Demi had lived so many different lives. She'd been raised in Australia and had been a young housewife in Dubai before moving to Brighton. Demi had a regular job at an insurance company and she was close to her family. She was thriving, independent and happy. She was a walking embodiment of the possibilities of being at home with yourself and seemed to have all the things I thought I'd lose if I came out as trans. There's a magic in being extraordinary, which she was in terms of her beauty, but there's a magic in being ordinary too. She wasn't a celebrity, she wasn't a performer, she didn't lead a life that was by any means excessively glamorous. She got up and went to work in the morning, clocked out at five and had fun at the weekend.

Over the months that followed we became inseparable. I told her that I thought I might be trans and wanted to try using she/her pronouns. She began to refer to me affectionately as her daughter, or in her words, 'daughter dear'. Demi opened my eyes to an entire world of gender possibilities that I had no idea existed. Until this point, I had thought that if I transitioned, I would end up not being able to be part of the real world. I would be disenfranchised and forced to live in the shadows. It made me feel hopeful, that she was just out in the light being who she wanted to be. She made me feel closer to my instinctive self to the extent that my gender dysphoria was alleviated whenever I was around her. I was starting to connect the dots as to why I had felt so at odds with my body, my perceived masculinity, my gender identity and sexuality throughout my life. I wanted to learn more, I wanted to understand not only what was possible, but what it meant to be trans. Demi helped to educate me on the history of our community through films, books and stories. She shared advice and tips on how I could feminise my appearance, and became a true confidante, the first person I could be completely open with about my identity and not feel like I was being judged, dehumanised or misunderstood.

Up to that point I just wasn't exposed to many, if any, transgender success stories or role models. I couldn't see myself reflected anywhere. The only public figures I knew of at the time were the few trans women on British television in the late 1990s and early 2000s, such as the winner of the 1998 Eurovision Song Contest, Dana International, who was subjected to endless transphobic media harassment. Then there was the character of Hayley Cropper in British soap

Coronation Street, who, as positive as the character was, wasn't played by a transgender actor and was in no way relatable to me as an eleven-year-old, mixed-race, Black kid. *Big Brother* winner, Nadia Almada, won the hearts of the nation in 2004, but was later torn to shreds by the tabloids, outed and shamed as an ex-sex worker. There was the late Miriam Rivera, who featured in a reality show called *There's Something About Miriam* in 2004, in which six young single men competed for her affection, bachelorette-style, unaware that she was, as the tabloids would distastefully put it at that time, 'born a man'. The male contestants of the show then went on to launch a lawsuit against the producers for 'inflicting psychological and emotional damage, and conspiracy to commit sexual assault because they were not made aware of Miriam's circumstances'.

Trans women in the media were portrayed as two-dimensional tabloid spectacles, in an effort to shift papers on a slow news day, with a 'Sex swap shock' or 'She's got a secret, lads' headline. They were monsterised or fetishised depending on how sexy people found them. At the time I thought, 'I don't want to be like those women,' but what I really meant was 'I don't want to go through what they went through.' There was only one trans narrative in the mainstream and that was tragedy.

While I didn't especially want a job at an insurance company like Demi, I loved the fact that she could live the low-key life of her choosing. Normality is something other people take for granted. For trans folk, normality is a privilege, often contingent on how well we 'pass' for cisgender in the eyes of wider society. It dictates our safety in public spaces, our professional opportunities and ultimately, our ability to move through the world without being consistently othered or questioned on the basis of our transness. This should not be the case, yet it still unfortunately is.

The workplace is often not particularly welcoming to trans people who do not 'pass' in the eyes of potential employers, or to people who want to transition. Yes, there are laws in place to protect us, but are people aware of those laws? Do they act accordingly? In the UK in 2022, the rate of unemployment within the transgender community is estimated to be 15 per cent, which is three times the unemployment rate of the population as a whole. A report from leading UK LGBT charity Stonewall found that 33 per cent of employers admitted that they would be 'less likely' to hire someone if they were transgender, with 43 per cent stating that they were 'unsure' whether they would knowingly hire a worker who is trans. There are ways to get around those laws, and no law is going to prevent you from feeling unwelcome.

Whenever I had a question about anything gender-related that I was spiralling about, Demi would say 'anything's doable'. There were times when I really needed to hear that. She'd show me pictures of her life before she transitioned; now she looked a world away from how she looked then. It gave me hope for my own transition, that I shouldn't feel discouraged or limited by the 'maleness' of my physique, and reminded me that it isn't all about the physical. 'You shouldn't make this decision in terms of being desired,' she told me. 'It's about who you are, not how others see you.' She asked me clarifying questions, urging me to look into my future, to see myself beyond the fleeting experience of youth. 'Would you rather be an old man or an ugly old woman? Don't transition on the basis of beauty,' she said. That really shed light on it for me. What direction did I want my life to go in? What did I want for the future version of myself? There is, in my experience, no singular defining moment when you come to realise that you're trans. I always knew, if subconsciously. But meeting Demi fast-forwarded the process of understanding myself. Her presence gave me a safe space to interrogate my feelings, my hopes and fears. Her insistence that I educate myself on transgender history and culture ignited my sense of pride. The more I saw her thrive, the more I allowed myself to accept that I was trans.

Demi transcended everything I believed to be true about being trans. She opened my mind to the possibility that I could also transcend what I thought trans people could be. She opened my mind to the reality of it, urging me to unpick the internalised transphobic thought patterns that had been spun in self–hatred. My world was led by people's small-minded ideas of what being trans meant. Everything I'd been feeling close to was trans; I just hadn't said it aloud.

Just seeing her made me realise that being trans is not just visually beautiful, it's a pathway to being able to feel whole and live your life in a way that feels authentic. Seeing someone living authentically was the permission I needed to help me do the same.

Demi was my first real role model and I owe her so much. There were so many kindnesses I failed to notice at the time. She was always cooking, it seemed to me, and then insisting that she'd made too much chicken soup for herself and that I must take some home. I later realised that she'd been cooking because she wanted me to eat. Much to my delight, she lived about five minutes away from me and whenever things felt like they were too much, I'd pop across the road. When I had to leave, I felt like I was going back into the darkness.

And then, suddenly one day, Demi disappeared. I was scared and confused because up to this point we spoke all the time. Nothing like this had ever happened before. Weeks passed and I didn't know what to think or how to feel. This incredible person with whom I had been so vulnerable, who had helped improve the state of my mental health, who I had shared parts of myself with that I hadn't with anyone else, was no longer there. I could feel myself free-falling, my thoughts were racing again and I wasn't eating enough. I hadn't realised it, but with my increased alcohol consumption, my antidepressants had stopped working and my mind was beginning to spiral deep into self-destruction.

I had started living on one bowl of cereal per day, black coffee and slimming pills. I was sleeping most of the day, drinking excessively and taking drugs at night. Anything to numb myself. I wanted to escape from the constant dull ache of depression, and the irrational racing thoughts that brought on my anxiety. It worked for a short while, until I started to become visibly unwell. My skin broke out all over my body, my hair started to fall out, I lost my libido completely and had little to no energy or motivation to attend university classes. I became reclusive, only leaving the house at night. I had so much sadness, anger and confusion inside of me, more than I knew what to do with, so I took it all out on myself. I felt like I had been abandoned at my most vulnerable, as if I was a burden no longer worth bearing. A month passed and I received an email from Dr Jess Moriarty, my creative writing lecturer, to ask why I hadn't been attending her lectures and could I come to her office to discuss it with her. I told her that I wasn't well and booked in a slot to see her on campus. Her email probably saved my life.

When I got to her office I instantly broke down in tears, trying to explain everything that had happened in my life before Brighton. How I would seek out validation from older men and end up in situations that would wind up with me feeling worse about myself. I told her about where I grew up, about my relationship with my dad and how I thought everything would be better in Brighton, but how it had all seemed to follow me. I wasn't ready to tell her about my gender identity or Demi's disappearance. But from that point on, Jess helped me to start helping myself. She encouraged me to own the hurt I was feeling and put it into my creative writing work. She helped me to develop the skills that I now use every day in writing to connect with others. If it wasn't for those meetings in Jess's office, if it wasn't for the kindness, understanding and patience that she showed me when I needed it, I probably wouldn't be here today. Due to missing so many lectures I had a lot of catching up to do, but I stayed as sober and clean as I could and started seeing a counsellor about my eating.

Demi got back in contact. She explained that she had been sexually assaulted by a stranger outside her home. Physically she was OK but the trauma had made her shut down. At the time I couldn't understand why she hadn't told me, when I had told her everything. I now realise that she must have felt the pressure of mentoring me, that she felt unable to share something so serious with someone who was battling their own demons. I didn't realise how unequal our relationship was back then, how much I leaned on her, to the point that she didn't feel she could lean on me when she needed to. I was heartbroken for her, but I was also in recovery myself and instead of coming together we became more and more distant. I pushed any thought of being trans and any plans of transitioning out of my head. I didn't feel strong enough or wise enough to go through this right now, and especially not on my own. I wasn't ready to talk to anyone about it. So, I pushed it down, deep down and tried to keep on living 'as a boy'.

★

I was struggling to hold it together, till one day I couldn't do it any longer. I had been to my first Pride parade in my first year at university and having never been in such a stunningly joyous environment before, I'd almost been overwhelmed, too excited to register it. This year I was determined to enjoy every moment.

Things didn't go according to plan. A group of friends and I started the day at the flat I shared with Jodie, a bubbly, 5ft 2in, half-Egyptian friend who I met on my course. We were drinking and all a little buzzed when one of them pulled out a peyote – a hallucinogenic Mexican cactus – to really get the mood going. It was not something I'd tried before, not that I took much convincing. About ten minutes after we'd taken it, the phone rings and it's my mother calling to tell me that my grandmother has died, and also the family dog. It wasn't the news you wanted straight after taking a hallucinogen and I didn't even really register it, let alone react in the moment. It was when we got to Pride and the hallucinations began that the effect sank in. The peyote opened up a Pandora's box where all the distress I was feeling inside began to manifest as hallucinations. I'd been hurting myself by not eating, sometimes cutting myself, sometimes burning the soles of my feet with heated utensils. I grew increasingly anxious at Pride – I felt like someone was watching me over my shoulder but when I looked there was no one there. The amount of people there didn't feel festive and celebratory as I'd hoped; it felt scary and overwhelming. I took my high heels off and began to walk home barefoot without telling my friends, who soon noticed I'd gone missing and started looking for me. Before they were able to find me, all hell broke loose.

When I got to the flat, I got a bread knife out of the cupboard and cut my wrist. My best friend Tommy showed up at the flat soon after and saw my wrist bandaged in a towel, though I refused to talk about it and asked as cheerfully as possible if anyone wanted a cup of tea. He followed the blood and found the knife I'd hidden down the back of the bed. I admitted to him that I'd hurt myself, but I refused to go to the hospital or get help and there wasn't much he could do.

After that incident I kept cutting myself, but privately, without causing obvious alarm. The pain I was feeling hadn't lessened though, it was just bottled up. One day I cut all my hair off with a pair of scissors. I wasn't on drugs or anything but I could feel that I was losing control of my mind. Every other time I'd suffered with poor mental health, my self-harm had been a method of control – the cutting, the starving – but to lose control of my mind really scared me.

When I cut off my hair, I climbed out onto a window ledge and it was there, wondering whether to jump, that I snapped out of it. The window was on the first floor and I don't even know what I wanted – to die? to hurt myself badly? I just knew I wasn't in charge any longer and the thought of it terrified me.

I called the police on myself. They came to my flat and asked me if I'd kill myself if they left. I told them I didn't know, so they took me to the station and put me in a cell for ten hours for my own protection. Being locked up was a new kind of rock bottom. The police called a mental-health specialist to assess me to see whether I should be admitted to a facility. I told him everything about how I was feeling, about my gender dysmorphia, my self-harm, that my dearest friend and the only person I'd ever connected with in such a way had left my life, about a volatile relationship with an ex-boyfriend and my relationship with my family. He told me I was experiencing extreme mental distress and trauma but that I was not suicidal and that if I went to a facility, it would destroy my future. He said I seemed intelligent and lucid and that I was at university and could go on to do things with my life and that what I needed was help, but not in the form of institutionalisation. Having said this, he handed me a few leaflets. He didn't refer me to another doctor or explain anything about any other resources. Being handed some leaflets after you've chopped off your hair with some kitchen scissors and almost jumped out of a window wasn't what I needed. I knew I'd lost control of myself that day and I didn't want to be alone in case it happened again.

I stopped cutting myself for a while after this incident because it had scared me so much, but my eating disorder galloped along. It felt different though, as if I'd gone from trying to control myself to wanting to punish myself. I'd always thought suicide was a selfish thing to do, to check out of life leaving your loved ones to suffer your loss. I could see now that there was nothing selfish about it and that mental illness is often beyond logic and reason. I understand now that suicide deserves complete compassion and that it happens in a place beyond desperation.

I got through university and graduated with a 2:1. I'd like to think if I hadn't been so depressed I might have done better.

★

When my university era came to a close, I started putting some serious, albeit overdue, thought into a strategy for my professional career. I'd always been drawn to the creativity and freedom of the fashion industry, so I applied for some entry-level PR positions. After a few months of interviews, I landed a role at a luxury boutique firm in Brighton where I began to learn the ropes, and was then offered a better paid internship at one of the largest and most prestigious fashion and beauty PR agencies in London. Mum had encouraged me to move back home for a few months while I acclimatised to London working life. My father and I pretty much continued to ignore each other, but this was made easier by me hardly ever being there. Getting up at 6am for the daily commute, I was at work from 8am to 8pm and just came home to sleep. My role put me in charge of the agency's press cuttings, requiring me to scan and file brand coverage in the papers and magazines for the account executives. I worked hard and diligently, which three months later led to a permanent job offer. I was promoted to account executive and could finally afford a room in a flat share, so off to London I moved. I worked in that role for three years, as the intermediary between magazines and stylists. If *Vogue*, say, wanted to put Calvin Klein underwear or a pair of Puma trainers in a photoshoot, they would come to me and I would lend them the product in return for coverage in the publication.

Fashion PR felt different from what I expected, less creative, less inclusive. I had reverted to my birth name at work and found myself not taking much pride in my personal style, often wearing a simple pair of jeans and a T-shirt if I wasn't required to see a client. I knew this wasn't the wholeness of me, but I didn't feel that this was an environment where the real visual me would be understood or encouraged. I didn't want to be the talking point in the office.

The idea of transitioning while at work felt like a battle too big to endure and I wasn't sure of what my legal protections were, if any. In fact, the Equalities Act protecting people from being sacked for being trans was passed in 2010, the year that I decided to leave. I was trying hard to get ahead, often working later than I had to and taking on additional tasks. I was doing well, but the catty office culture between the execs made it hard to keep myself motivated and enthusiastic about being there.

As I began to move up the ranks of the agency, I wasn't spending my evenings with my co-workers;

I was in the thick of London's queer nightlife, carving out a space for myself there. I was done with living to work, I wanted to live, period. So, every Friday evening after work, I headed over to King's Cross and the London Sound Academy, where I took DJ lessons. Thankfully my networking had paid off and I quickly booked some weekly residencies, spinning at legendary Soho venues: Heaven, Madame JoJo's and the Shadow Lounge. DJing helped me to build back some of the confidence that I had lost while working in fashion. I'd become used to making myself small again. It was in these Soho venues and on these dance floors, among Soho's drag performers, nightlife eccentrics, showgirls, club kids, sex workers and go-go boys that I began to regain my sense of community and identity. Transitioning began to feel like more of a possibility and I felt alive again, so I started taking a few more steps towards it, like having laser hair removal on my face and legs, baby steps to help me get closer to my eventual goal.

While my night-time self was blossoming, I was struggling at my day job. Once the dust had settled after the recession, the agency had taken on many more clients, with fewer execs to look after them following a brutal wave of cuts and layoffs. I was now looking after some very big accounts, and the work seemed endless, while there was little or no emotional support from senior staff. My manager and I didn't get along. I don't know if it was the pressure that we were both under, or whether she just didn't want me on her team.

One day she was off sick so I had to look through her correspondence to find an email to a client. While scrolling I saw my name being mentioned, so naturally I read it. My heart sank when I found that she was talking about me to our account director in a way that was misrepresentative of my character, calling me lazy and undedicated to the role. The truth is, I was struggling professionally and emotionally, with more clients and tasks than I could handle, working with a manager who treated me like dirt every day of the week. I was quickly running out of steam, experiencing professional burnout but not knowing that burnout was even a thing.

That afternoon I realised how unhappy and unfulfilled I was working there. As a last resort I decided to speak to the owner of the company citing my concerns about our workload, well-being and my personal working relationship with my manager. Their response was dismissive and cold: 'These are the times that we are in, we're all under pressure, and respectfully, what do you expect her to do? Give you a hug?'

I handed in my resignation that evening. I'd reached breaking point. It had become abundantly clear that this was an unsustainable and unhealthy environment for me to be in. No pay cheque is worth sacrificing the health of your soul, and that is what it was starting to feel like. I had a few months' savings in the bank, just enough to scrape by. Looking back now, I was extremely naïve when it came to my finances, but I'm glad that I took the jump and chased my happiness. Perhaps it worked in my favour, not being so concerned with money and material things. It was a risk that helped me transition out of that era of putting my whole life on pause. It forced me to fully focus on what I wanted for my future, what would truly make me happy, and I'm beyond thankful to my past self for prioritising that above all else.

Looking back at that time, I'm so proud of myself for how hard I hustled after leaving the agency. I wasn't waiting for any opportunities to come to me, I was making them happen and living on my own terms. During the daytime I did part-time receptionist work at an art gallery, I was a photographer's assistant, I took bookings at a restaurant and worked at a magazine. In the evenings I had found more nightlife opportunities in the West End. It was still very much the heyday of Soho, at a time when it was full of neon lights, sex shops, seedy glamour and hedonistic character. I was being seen at the right places, hosting a lot of cool parties and quickly becoming referred to as something of a queer scene It Girl. Although I wasn't making much actual money and didn't have any real access to the lifestyle that many of the guests attending the parties had, I didn't really care. I could feel that it was all leading to something.

★

I started taking hormones at twenty-three years old. In those early days I didn't know what I was doing, really; there wasn't much in the way of information on the internet about how to transition; it was all pretty much word of mouth. Soho was always very trans; it had little by way of racial diversity but I felt at home in its anything-goes mentality regarding self-expression. I found my access to the trans community there and learned a lot about the reality of being a trans person in the UK from other girls at parties. Soho was a crash course in glamorous excess, faking it until you make it and surviving by any means possible. I learned that as I'd suspected, trans people are not employed as easily as our cisgender counterparts, and this pushes many of us into sex work as a matter of survival. The number of trans women I've known who've had to do this is ridiculous.

I believe that sex work is work and should be decriminalised so that workers are safer and protected under the law. Many people go into sex work willingly, but many do not; it is a means of survival within a society that has depleted their options, a society that is shutting them out and denying them opportunity. The number of trans women I've known take their own lives or have their lives taken by accidental drug overdoses or violent clients, is abhorrent and heart-breaking. Criminalising sex work, much like criminalising drugs or abortion, doesn't stop it from happening; it forces people into dangerous situations that are unregulated and places the blame on the vulnerable while ignoring the wider issues within society.

In 2011 I somewhat stumbled into modelling. I'd always had an interest in it but I never thought that I looked the way a model could or should look. I hadn't seen many people who looked like me on magazine covers or on runways to show me otherwise. I had been posting images of myself on social media when promoting the events that I was hosting and some of them had caught the eye of Lebanese couture designer Ziad Ghanem. One morning I got a frantic call from his casting director, as a model hadn't shown up for a look-book-shoot. He asked if I could jump in a cab straight away to take her place and I guess that's how I shot my first campaign!

On set I was insecure about my body, blagging my way through with Tyra Banks's advice on *America's Next Top Model* as my only reference on how to pose. It's one thing knowing when an image looks good in a magazine; it's a whole other thing knowing how to model. Although they weren't aware of my eating disorder, my relationship with anorexia wasn't exactly discouraged. It was a time when thin was most definitely in and I had to be tiny if I wanted to fit into the couture. Although I didn't have much experience or understanding about modelling, I started working with Ziad more. I was booked for two campaigns and a show, which led to me shooting a magazine editorial by renowned portrait photographer David Bailey.

I don't think people realise how closely entwined the fashion industry and London nightlife were back then. You often just had to be at the right party, in the right look, shot by the right photographer, to catch the right person's eye, and it could potentially change everything. I'd never approach anyone famous while at work, but now and again someone would notice me and I'd end up in VIP all night, being introduced to influential people within the industry and sometimes getting a modelling job from it. A lot of my early career was really a case of being in the right place at the right time, embracing the happy accidents and making the most of every moment.

★

Everybody who works in fashion has an aesthetic and a niche. As a trans person in 2011 I knew that my time hadn't yet come. I didn't have the looks of a runway model; I didn't have the height for high fashion, the skin for beauty or the cis-normative look for it either. I knew that if I wanted to do this, I would have to create my own lane. At the time, when you were hired as a model you really didn't get to talk. But with the emergence of social media influencing, you did. While I didn't have an especially large following on social media, I had more than most other trans people in the UK and wanted to use it as an opportunity to be a voice for my community. I wanted to plug into this medium and use my growing platform to bridge fashion, beauty, modelling, politics, my lived experience and my opinion. I started being mindful of what I was posting and showing the parts of me that I wanted both the industry and the public to see.

This was a time when you strictly didn't talk about politics at most parties; you made small talk and had fun, you drank, you took drugs, you looked happy. If you were too opinionated, people wouldn't invite you because you were deemed a vibe kill. Now you can't get away from it. Now you're more likely to have political conversations on a night out and less likely to engage with people with opposite political opinions, often to avoid judgement or conflict. That's a transitional moment in itself – we have changed from avoiding discussing politics and money to actively talking about both of these things to a greater degree. For Black and brown and queer people, not talking about these things plays into our own oppression, since now the only people who are comfortable with them not being spoken about are the ones who like the system just as it is. Blending fashion, beauty, politics and my opinion felt liberating and purposeful. I began to feel like a whole person with a story that could help enact change and empower others, not just a good-time girl in a fab pair of heels smiling for the camera.

What most people who aren't trans or don't know any trans people aren't aware of, is that the process for medically transitioning is painfully slow, frustrating, invasive and complicated. It took me a long time to summon the courage to speak to my GP about beginning my medical transition. I'd heard so many horror stories about doctors trying to talk trans women out of beginning hormones, encouraging conversion therapy or outright refusing to treat or refer them. All doctors take a Hippocratic oath to do no harm and treat everybody as equals, but in practice this simply isn't the case. I'd heard of religious GPs, for example, referring to being trans as a mental illness, refusing to treat trans patients because of their personal faith and recommending private prayer or prayer groups, essentially conversion therapy (which is still completely legal).

Being aware of all these narratives, I went into my initial consultation ready to fight for my healthcare and I wasn't going to leave without a referral. 'I'm transgender, I'm already taking hormones and living as a woman, I need you to refer me to a specialist *today.*'

My GP looked at me with confusion, probably because I had come in a little hot – not that it was entirely unreasonable or unwarranted. He responded, 'I'm going to be honest with you, I've never met a trans person before, so I'm going to have to ask Google.' I was almost relieved that he was hapless on the subject rather than bigoted, but nevertheless, this was my personal introduction to just how poorly NHS staff are trained when it comes to transgender healthcare. But when it came to the crunch, I'd rather have someone uninformed and helpful, than someone bigoted and harmful. He proceeded to ask me a series of gender-related questions and referred me to a psychiatrist in East London, who would then diagnose me with gender dysphoria and refer me to the Charing Cross Gender Identity Clinic.

★

The UK transgender healthcare system is broken. It's overwhelmed, underfunded and outdated. It took twelve months for my first appointment at the GI clinic to arrive, which is small fry considering that today the waiting list is now a minimum of five years from referral, with approximately 2,702 – and rising – trans people waiting for their first assessment on the NHS.

In my first appointment I met with a counsellor who assessed my mental state. Their job is essentially to decide whether you are ready to transition and to see whether you meet specific criteria to be living in the gender you identify as. I was wearing trousers at the time, and he asked me if I was wearing women's clothes, as if women don't wear trousers or jeans or suits, as if it would somehow render me less trans if I was wearing different garments. I remember feeling infuriated that this cisgender white man with a notepad was asking me to fulfil his narrow notion of womanhood, that he had power over my future in that way. I was defensive and possibly borderline rude to the man because I was being treated as if I was mentally ill rather than being believed to be who I said I was. It felt like I was constantly being asked to prove that I deserved to be there, like people were checking off their boxes on a list to quantify how trans I was. In those early appointments I felt like they were trying to catch me out, as if saying something wrong would mean I wouldn't be able to access this healthcare that I desperately needed.

Currently the process is that after your appointment at the GI Clinic, you're meant to live in the gender you identify as for two years before you're given your first hormones. This is completely unrealistic and traumatising and not something most trans people adhere to. It has been devised very much from the perspective of a cis person who thinks that perhaps trans people just aren't sure of what they want. Do they not think years of deliberation have led them to this choice? If someone has made the decision to transition, they couldn't be surer. In the UK, it was found that out of 3,398 attendees of a gender identity clinic, only sixteen attendees – 0.47 per cent – experienced gender transition regret. However even fewer of these attendees made the decision to detransition.

Some trans people are able to get a breast augmentation on the NHS if they've had a severe lack of breast growth from hormones after two years, but we aren't given access to facial feminisation surgery, which is what a lot of trans people actually want. The focus is on genitalia, which again upholds the idea of binary sex, that trans women who don't have sexual reassignment surgery aren't trans women and shouldn't be allowed in women's spaces. None of us is the sum of our genitalia. Should we want it, we should be helped with what people see – our faces – because for a lot of people that's what's going to alleviate their gender dysphoria. That's what's going to give trans people the confidence to feel at home in themselves, to be part of the workplace, to face the world, to feel the gender euphoria accessed with being able to see yourself reflected in the mirror and with others seeing you as you wish to be seen.

In the early stages of a gender transition, you're stuck in this place between where you were and where you want to be. At this stage, I found it really difficult to be in public – it felt like I was on display all the time. For a lot of people I was considered a sideshow. People would talk behind their hands and take pictures of me on their phone. I would hear people on the street jeering and laughing, sometimes saying 'it's a tranny' deliberately within earshot, ushering their children away from me. Being illuminated on the Tube made me all the more visible. I would sit there with a racing heartbeat, in a cold sweat, wondering if I'd be beaten up by those looking at me with fixed stares of disdain, wondering whether anyone would intervene or even want to. I only felt comfortable in nightlife.

I'd briefly taken a job at a clothing store in Soho where I thought people might be less conservative, but sometimes customers would laugh at me in my place of work. They'd say they didn't want to be served by me, saying 'I can't believe that "this" is working at the counter' to my co-workers. I quit because I was embarrassed that this kept happening and that I had to keep drawing attention, even sympathy, from my co-workers in this way. When something keeps happening, you do start to wonder if you're the problem. I left that job and stuck to nightlife. Eventually the abuse on the street got so bad that I was living off delivery food apps and only leaving the house when the sun went down.

This went on for about three years of my early transition. As I started to look more and more like society's idea of a woman, I would now find myself being cat-called. I started to have a very strange relationship with the reactions to me on the street. I started navigating the paradox between danger and objectification. I would be pointed at and shouted at, spat at, told I shouldn't be near kids, treated like a monster, but also I would be followed by men who knew that I was trans but who would objectify me in ways that were extremely sexual. They would often assume that I was a sex worker or at least someone for them to easily fuck.

When I was cat-called I would think, do these people know I'm trans, because if they don't they may get very angry and this is how trans women, especially many Black trans women, end up being murdered. As I started to look more 'feminine', I also started confusing sexual objectification with validation. It meant that they found me desirable, they liked me. They were breadcrumbs of validation but it was more than I'd had before; being fetishised felt like genuine affection. Even now, now that I can move through the world not being bothered as much, even now when I'm cat-called on the street, I almost always freeze, thinking, will this man switch if he knows I'm trans, how will this man react upon knowing he's attracted to a trans woman? Or do they know I'm trans, and are they objectifying me for that?

I told my mum I was trans when I was twenty-six. By this point I had been on hormones for nearly four years. I couldn't hide it from her any longer, nor did I want to. At the time I was living in Stratford, East London and still working in nightlife, but my modelling career was beginning to pick up pace. I was anxious to tell her, because of how she responded to me coming out in my teens, but I hoped this time would be different: she'd grown so much since then in terms of embracing my sexuality.

Unfortunately, history repeated itself, and she completely panicked. My body was beginning to change. I could tell that she thought she was losing me. I tried reassuring her that it would never be that way, that she would be gaining a happy child instead of risking losing an unhappy one. But I felt like she wasn't listening, she wasn't engaging with me and she didn't understand. We didn't speak for a long while after this.

In the time that followed, I felt abandoned and lost. I'd found myself settling for less than I deserved across the board – what I was paid, how I was treated, how I was loved. I settled for scraps. Everything had started to take a wrong turn.

I had run myself into the ground in the pursuit of making a name for myself. Despite remaining ambitious and driven, I wasn't having fun at all. I had often taken drugs socially but now drugs had become a way to cope, to numb myself from being unhappy and unsupported. I was drinking a lot, often to the point of blackout. I felt deflated by my parents' abandonment, and by the unsupportive and unhealthy romantic relationships I was having. I was rapidly approaching my thirties and still living pay cheque to pay cheque, trying to keep my mental health from taking a complete nosedive in the way it had in the past.

★

It's often said that it isn't being trans that is especially difficult; it's other people's perceptions of our transness and the way that these feelings are projected onto us that for many makes life feel unliveable, that makes us feel unlovable. If I had had the opportunity to transition within a society that prioritised supporting trans folk, that cared about our safety, our health, our inclusion or employment, then it would have been a very different experience indeed. But we live in a society where the trans community is still treated as an inconvenience, an anomaly, an afterthought, an agenda or an issue. We are a community too small for governments to pander to, but big enough to exploit as a political pawn in the weaponisation of fear in the pursuit of potential votes. If we can't rely on the government to have progressive conversations about how transgender people can be safe, functioning and thriving members of society, then we should take it upon ourselves to be the change we want to see.

Until then we must recognise that Britain's transphobia is not happening in a vacuum; it is being exacerbated and encouraged by people in the most powerful positions of government, including Boris Johnson, who was Prime Minister for much of the time I was writing this book. Until we have a government that recognises the humanity of transgender individuals and that is willing to understand our needs and lived experiences, we will continue to face societal ostracism; we will continue to struggle; we will continue to die. Blood is quite literally on the UK Conservative government's hands.

Love

From an early age we are taught about love and relationships in relation to who we are perceived to be by those around us. The concept of love is often gendered and presented as a one-size-fits-all ticket to human fulfilment before we truly know what fulfils us.

Love is initially presented as a form of socialisation – we are encouraged to understand love through emulation, to mirror and relate to the forms of love that we see in the world immediately around us. We are not only taught by society *who* to love, but also *how* to love them depending on cultural gender roles, our perceived/expected heterosexuality and first-hand demonstrations of love from within our family units. It is here that we not only first learn how to love, but also how to be loved and how to accept love.

Growing up gay meant no carefree, whirlwind, coming-of-age high-school romances. Growing up gay meant that it seemed there was no one else who was gay for miles around, even though there was. Growing up gay meant not being able to be open about who you truly had feelings for, when asked 'Who do you fancy?' Growing up gay meant giving your straight friends relationship advice, with no point of reference but what you'd seen on TV and in movies. Growing up gay meant that some adults who suspected that you might be gay uninvited you from their homes and preferred you not to play with their kids at school. Growing up gay meant not hearing any of your favourite pop stars sing about same-sex love, even though many of them were also gay themselves. Growing up gay meant averting your eyes whenever anything gay came on the television when watching with your family. Growing up gay meant always deleting the internet browser history on the family computer and feeling a lightning bolt of terror strike in your chest, any time your parents raised it over dinner. Growing up gay meant waiting eighteen years to find queer love, only to limit it to the rigid boundaries of heteronormativity. Growing up gay meant that your homophobic school bully was most likely also gay, but too scared to come out because of the toxic environment that you both had to navigate, so they took it out on you, the person who embodied what the world taught them to hate about themselves.

The biggest hurdle that I faced before I began living authentically, was my fear of potentially being alone as a consequence. I feared being alone; I didn't see being alone as strong or something that could be by choice. To be partnered meant that I was worth being invested in, to be partnered meant that it was possible for someone to love the parts of me that I didn't love myself. But as I eventually realised, you can't hate yourself into someone else loving you. It took me a long time to realise this.

It's one thing knowing about the importance of self-love. It's another thing feeling, owning and exercising it after an adolescence where society made you feel that you didn't deserve to be loved. It's easier to believe that one day someone is going to miraculously appear, sweep you off your feet and make everything better, than it is to see yourself as your own hero. But the easier strategy for coping with our trauma doesn't always make for the most effective solution, when the reality is that nobody can heal your trauma except you.

Most of us would rather date through our wants rather than our needs. These wants often take the form of social ideals that we have been led to believe will fulfil us, rather than the needs that require us to take a deeper look beneath the surface, to interrogate our attractions and explore our own relationships with the social, gender and relationship norms that we have been exposed to from an early age. Most of us would rather change ourselves to fit the status quo when it comes to relationships, than do the work to discover what it is that we actually need from a partner and therefore to be able to identify someone who can fulfill these needs. We are more likely to project these wants when dating a potential partner than communicate what it is that we actually need from them. This leads the dynamic to exist in a vacuum where neither party feels fulfilled due to lack of communication and the conflation of wants and needs. Looking back at my dating history, it's now clear to me that as my sense of self-love evolved, so did the kinds of people that I let into my life. I notice that partnerships became much more of a conscious choice, rather than a spontaneous fulfilment of validation. In my teens I dated older men because I felt that it validated my sexuality. As a young adult I dated men that I thought I could fix or help, as a way of avoiding healing or helping myself. During the early days of my transition, I dated masculine cisgender heterosexual men to uphold my physical sense of self to the world around me. The common pattern throughout these three eras was that I had no control over my romantic narrative, because I had no control over my internal narrative.

★

My first crush was on my primary-school bully. He would be aggressive and confrontational to other children too, and sometimes to the staff, but I was the one he paid the most attention to. I remember being on a bus with him once after I'd had a vaccination that had left me with a bump on my arm. He punched me so hard, the bump exploded. At this point in my life, I wasn't really being bullied for anything in particular. Occasionally I would have a kid repeat some racist insults that they must have overheard their parents saying, or they would comment on the fact that I was 'lanky' or 'girly'.

Curious as to why he disliked everyone this much, I started leaving him letters in his classroom tray where we kept our notebooks, stationery and lunchboxes. He started writing back to me even though we didn't speak in person. I remember that he would say how he felt emotionally, but would never allude to why. One day his mother found the letters in his backpack. The next morning, she burst into the form room, tightly grasping the top of his arm in one hand and the letters in the other. Spitting with rage, she called me, an eight-year-old child, every homophobic name under the sun. I didn't understand half of them till high school when other kids were calling me those names. She told me her son was forbidden from being friends with someone like me. This was my first experience of feeling that attraction to the same sex was unnatural and punishable, that loving someone of the same sex was wrong.

It's taken me a long time to realise that my trauma doesn't just exist within my memories, it has an impact on my relationships with others. If left unchecked it can dictate what relationships I end up in, acting as an invisible lighthouse for narcissists and emotional abusers, who benefit from a partner unaware of the extent of their own emotional wounds. Being conscious of our trauma, and recognising how it unavoidably manifests itself within our approach to romantic and platonic relations, allows us to strategise our connections. It helps us to recognise patterns, set boundaries, take heed of red flags and ultimately aim higher.

Transitioning out of unconscious trauma into conscious healing is much more than being in tune with our feelings. It's about looking at the choices we make, who we choose to have close to us, how they came into our lives and why we choose to keep them there. It's about recognising repetitive behavioural patterns, identifying the place in which our desire for validation is rooted and reconfiguring these aspects in a way that fosters positive, sustainable and consistent change within our lives. As a child I never thought that I would find myself within an abusive relationship, let alone multiple abusive relationships. That was something that happened to weak women, other women, it couldn't possibly happen to someone like me. That's how early I internalised that misogynistic narrative. In actuality, abusive partners happen to the strongest of people. They are specialists in manipulation and an abuser can always recognise trauma in a victim masquerading as need. My 'need' was attached to the isolation that I felt throughout my adolescence.

I wanted to be in love. I was willing to overlook red flags for that. I was willing to lose friends over the men that I let into my life for that. It is possible to break the chains of a trauma bond, but you have to realise how you got there, recognise that none of it is your fault and then get out of your own way. Deny them access to the part of you that remains unhealed, embrace that part and begin your journey into self-love and self-understanding. Then you may get the love you truly deserve, not the love you think you deserve. It's challenging for anyone to love themselves under the false value system of the patriarchy, and for me it's been perhaps my slowest, hardest, most meaningful transition.

I started questioning the role of the patriarchy in my transition right at the start of the process. I was trying to work out why I found such immense comfort in being desirable to men. To be honest, I still struggle with it. Living under the patriarchy, I'm continuously trying to unpick and understand love, to pull apart my interests and attractions and ask myself where they've come from. I was very aware of it when I first started dating as a trans person. At the beginning of my transition, I didn't look how I wanted to look, and also I didn't feel as if I looked how society wanted me to look.

I was being told all these things during my transition – false gender binaries about how femininity is an integral part of being a woman. The opposite of that, then, is masculinity. I thought that I needed a hypermasculine man to see my femininity in order to corroborate my womanhood, to make it feel real. I attached the validity of my gender identity to who I was dating. If men wanted me, I passed the test. It was beyond being trans and wanting to look feminine. I could now be judged like other women.

All women are judged by their appearance. As a society we don't see them in the same way if we consider them unattractive. We struggle to take them seriously in many professions. You only have to look at the way greying, rumpled men with visible ear hair present the news alongside sleek, groomed women. Would we not be able to absorb information if the women weren't so put together? A research study by the University of Washington suggests not, finding that women who are seen as 'conventionally attractive' by society and women who 'act feminine' are more likely to be believed when reporting sexual harassment. Unattractive women, however, are seen as 'uncredible', and their harasser is seen as deserving a lesser punishment.

So, I believed that in order to be safe, in order to be believed, in order to be helped, to be loved, in order for me to love myself, I needed to be attractive, I needed to be sexually appealing, I needed to be sexually active. I needed to have a man in my orbit for any of this to mean anything.

My inner child has always felt ugly. Like many others in early adulthood, I chased love. I mistook affection and attention for love, sought out validation and fell quickly in lust, confusing it for love. I was so very desperate for connection, that love became a pursuit of escapism. If someone else accepted me, then maybe I could accept myself. I wanted a physical sign that I was worthy of love, that it was possible to love me in the same way that I loved others. My context and my surroundings had taught me that I was monstrous and undesirable, but I was ugly by circumstance, not reality. But before I found this out, I sought refuge in glamour, a way of hiding in plain sight. A polished exterior with the right clothes, the right make-up, an expensive wig – it allows you to express yourself while also serving as a shield. You feel better about yourself when other people give their approval. This is how society works, it's normalised, internalised, considered the natural way of being.

However, you can run away from others, but when the abusive voice is your own, there's nowhere to run.

I've finally arrived at the conclusion that being glamorous for other people is depressing. I remember reading that Donatella Versace once said a dress is a weapon for women to get what they want. I don't think she was lying, and that's the sad part. Society tells women that we have to dress up for a situation to go our way. Once you've set that bar, there's the pressure to keep performing. If you're not glamorous all the time, you've 'let yourself go'. If you're not glamorous at all, then you're less likely to be believed. But glamour sometimes stops other people from seeing our depths. My image is the icing on the cake. It isn't the main part. If you eat just the icing, you're going to be sick. That's how I'd feel if I was expected to be glamorous all the time – sick.

I fell in love for the first time in my second year at university. Joey was a final-year art student and we'd been introduced by a mutual friend at a gay bar on the seafront. We had a drink later that week. I found him talented, mysterious, sexy, chaotic and, all in all, addictive. I enjoyed falling in love with him and did it very fast. It was the first time I'd felt truly wanted by anyone romantically – and I wanted him too, but not as much as I wanted to feel wanted.

At the end of a night out – and there were many – we'd usually be joined by his close friends and housemates and end up back at his flat, where they would continue the party with a bottle of brandy and a couple of grams of coke. Joey would often drink himself to the point where he couldn't speak or see and I would have to put him to bed. Then he'd sober up, plead for forgiveness. Next he would tell me I was overreacting. Then his mood would change and he'd be warm and full of compliments. Then we'd have wild passionate sex and I'd be hooked in again, addicted to the feeling of being wanted. Eventually his drinking got so bad that he would either not recognise me, looking straight through me in disgust, or he would become verbally abusive. That's when I began to feel unwanted. The eventual break-up left me sliding down a rabbit hole of self-harm and self-recrimination, culminating in a bout of anorexia.

I've been in a variety of relationships with men who were mentally and emotionally abusive. Initially I found there were very few men able to love the femininity within themselves and they would require a hypermasculine partner to be able to be queer without shame. And as I came into myself further, I found very few men capable of loving a trans woman in her wholeness. I so often found myself being loved in secret, or being sexually fetishised but disregarded in other ways.

Dating trans women often makes cisgender men see the patriarchy for what it is. They see that being with me would mean that they might also experience some of the transphobia that I experience in the streets. They have to give up some of their patriarchal power and the acceptance of the brotherhood that so many of them crave. They often have to grapple with their own masculinity. They may see transgender women as women, but society often does not, and so there is the question of how much it threatens them. In a world in which sexuality and gender aren't normalised as the sliding scale that they are, men are left to work out their internalised homophobia if they find themselves attracted to trans women. This often involves us experiencing violence or having control of some kind exerted over us to make us know our place. If we take up too much space and they had to involve us in the rest of their lives, such as introducing us to friends and family, they'd have to 'come out', and have conversations they don't want to have. Dating trans people brings internal struggles to the surface for our partners and we often end up paying the price for that, sometimes with our lives.

*

One night in 2010 after a DJ gig, I met up with my housemates for some drinks at the Joiner's Arms, a now defunct, but legendary pub in London's Shoreditch. By the time that I got there, everyone was pretty buzzed. I'd sobered up in the cab ride over from Soho, so I ordered some shots at the bar to play catch-up. At the beginning of my transition, I was taking a brand of hormone replacement therapy (HRT) called Premarin, which always seemed to send me left when I drank alcohol, especially on a big night out. I don't remember much of that night other than shots at the bar, dancing with my flatmate Hasan and getting talking to a man that I met in the smoking area. I subsequently took him home and had a one-night stand with him.

He was about 5ft 10in with a muscular build. I can't remember his name; I think I've mentally blocked it out, like I have his face over the years. I don't remember hooking up with him as such; we'd both had a lot to drink, but it was afterwards when we were lying in bed that things started to come into focus and I realised that something wasn't right. He told me that I was the first trans girl that he had been with, insisted that he wasn't gay and that we needed to keep what had happened between us. I assured him our night together would stay between us and that his sexuality was none of my business as we'd just met. As it was, I'd probably chosen him based on his masculinity giving me the affirmation I'd desired then.

I had no intention of seeing him again. But something felt off – and I couldn't tell what it was entirely. He asked to stay, saying that he wanted to wake up with me, but eventually he left. I felt an immediate sense of relief as soon as the door closed behind him, even though nothing specific happened that I could put my finger on. Somehow it felt like I'd dodged a bullet. For lack of a better turn of phrase, he gave me the creeps.

The following morning, I received a text message from him. I didn't remember giving him my number. It said 'Will you be my girlfriend?' I didn't text him back, not knowing how to say no and unable to shake my unease at him having been in my house. At work I turned my phone off and put it in my locker. I tried not to read too much into it – I worked in nightlife, I'd seen some shit and this was far from the strangest. When I turned my phone on again in my lunch break, I'd received a dozen text messages – each growing progressively angrier and more paranoid than the last – and on top of this, fifteen missed calls. Conditioned to be apologetic and not assert myself unduly, I messaged him to apologise and explain that I'd been at work. I then said as gently as possible that I wasn't able to commit to a relationship at that time. His responses came in a flurry. Days went by but the calls and texts didn't stop. The intense tone remained even when they grew less frequent. I changed my number.

A couple of months passed without my hearing from him. I'd put it out of my mind and was absorbed in my work anyway. One day I was walking to my local Tube station in Bow and he was there, standing straight in front of me. I froze and eventually managed to say hello. He grabbed my arm and quickly led me out of the station towards an alley around the back. He looked around to see if anyone saw us and said, 'Don't you ever talk to me in public, I should kill you for that.' He pushed me against the wall and walked away. I stopped using headphones in public after that, and tried to be as vigilant as possible of my surroundings.

He started showing up at my house. Thankfully I was never there when this happened, but he would interrogate my flatmates as to my whereabouts. I didn't think that stalking was something that even happened to 'normal people', and it took me some time to accept that that was what was happening. For three months he kept showing up at the door, while I managed not to be there or to avoid him every time. Once I saw him walking around the neighbourhood and beat a retreat.

At five o'clock one morning I heard a banging at the door and I thought perhaps one of my flatmates had forgotten their keys. I opened the door on the latch to check and before I could quickly close it, he kicked it down. My housemate Hasan was asleep upstairs, but he told me that if I screamed for help, he'd kill me. He led me to my room, closed the door and held me captive there for two hours, brutally raping me. At moments I looked around the room wondering if I could hit him over the head with something heavy, but then thought about what it would look like for a Black trans woman to be found with a body in her house. He poured cocaine on me while he raped me, pushing it up my nose and forcing it in my mouth with his fingers. Eventually I apologised for resisting him, said I would be more co-operative and pointed to a silky nightie on a hanger on my wardrobe door, saying I'd put it on for him. The moment I got my opportunity, I bolted upstairs to Hasan's room and told him to call the police. He was gone before they arrived.

I was hesitant to report being raped – I knew how it looked. I knew there was very little chance of being believed, and I'd never trusted the police anyway. But I felt I had no choice. Unfortunately, many of my reservations about involving the police were realised. Throughout my physical examination in which every bruise, cut, scratch and mark on my body was recorded, there was so little consideration for my mental state.

I saw him once more at Madame JoJo's for a trans club night where I was working on the door. I was dressed up but I knew he recognised me. I let him into the venue hoping that the CCTV would pick up his face. I called the police as soon as he had gone downstairs and asked the security guards to hold him inside the venue, but they refused as the incident hadn't happened on the premises. Again, he escaped. I overheard my boss talking about it when they didn't think I was in earshot: 'So it was true then...', confirming my fears that I wasn't being believed by those I needed to believe me. I gave the case as much as I could; I told my case officer every possible detail, but the longer it went unsolved, the less hope I had that I would see any form of justice prevail. Despite being caught on CCTV and pictures of his face being plastered around Bow on 'wanted' posters, they never found him. I moved to South London a few weeks later and I never saw him again.

★

I was raped at twenty-three years old, right at the beginning of my transition, and as I've grown older, I've been able to contextualise it differently. My rapist wanted to punish me for his attraction to me. He was so ashamed of being attracted to trans women that he had dehumanised me enough to be able to rape me. He wanted my complete subordination in order to assert his power. I think I was wilfully ignorant of someone being capable of doing that. It's dictated how I've lived my life since. It's always in the back of my mind that the person I'm on a date with or sitting in a room with could perhaps be capable of this. It could be anybody, after all. I carry around the possibility of reliving that in my head and I probably always will.

Even though the attack was sexual in nature, it wasn't sex. Afterwards, it took away my full ability to engage sexually with people. I didn't enjoy sex because I couldn't separate it from being raped.

It's hard to feel empowered in your body again. I'd had eating issues before but they had been rooted in my trying to stem the masculinisation of my body and control my feelings. This made me hate my body in its totality. This had happened just as I'd made the huge decision to begin my gender transition and I'd even started to forget why I'd undertaken this act of love for myself.

I started entering relationships where my partners would exert mental and physical violence on me. The mental violence was worse because I couldn't see it happening at the time. I was entering into relationships with narcissists who would whittle me down and bring me to my knees. The trauma of being raped exacerbated my existing belief that people would only ever love me for a reason, that love wasn't unconditional. My parents wouldn't love me if I told them I was gay or trans, I thought, and so I felt like it was OK to be loved in part, for what I could be for someone. The idea of love coming easy and being deserved didn't feel at all true.

For years I went from one bad relationship to the next. They were all bad in different ways. Accessible conversations about trans love and ways of connecting are fairly recent, and it felt impossible to find anyone to exchange experiences with then. There was nothing to read or find online. It was only on hearing each other's stories in person that I could begin to see that we all carry the same type of shame – the shame that says maybe I am unlovable and maybe this is what I deserve. It becomes part of you. And you open yourself up to physical violence, name-calling, mind-games and gaslighting, to people that are withholding. It's like a sliding scale of violence that you end up enacting on yourself. The way I viewed myself was violent, and I was dehumanising myself by accepting these options.

★

I met James one night at a club in London. It was full of trans women, drag queens and conventionally attractive gay and bisexual, mostly masculine, men. It was one of those decadent places where anything might happen. Studio 54 vibes. He was tall and slender, with shoulder-length brown hair scraped back into a 90s Johnny Depp bun; everyone would notice him when he walked into a room. Looking back at it now, I'm able to see through it all: there was nothing original to him, not really. Even his sex appeal was a con, a curation of clichés, rehearsed and moulded around his own observations of what other people would find attractive, not an expression of his own personality or natural desirability. But I fell for it, hard.

We locked eyes the moment we saw each other and had a couple of drinks at the bar. I got pulled away to the dance floor and we lost each other in the club, but he later asked some mutual friends for my number and rang to ask me for a date the next week. I heavily romanticised the situation, desperately grateful that such a 'desirable man' should see my womanhood and treat me like a woman.

James was a typical narcissist. Narcissists are often extremely charming because their lives depend on it. It's easier and faster to get what you want when it comes with a winning smile and lashings of flattery. He was very extremely good at telling people what they wanted to hear. He knew how to manipulate young trans women. I would get endless promises of marriage, stability, children, somewhere where I could feel loved, safe and empowered. The reality is I never got any of that. All I got was his rather lacklustre parody of masculinity and the promises he dangled – that it would all be worth it. There was also the insinuation that I was never going to get this from anyone else and that I should be thankful for him seeing and accepting my womanhood, that really, my womanhood only existed in proximity to him. You only believe someone who tells you that no one but them would want you when you intrinsically believe that about yourself. Eventually he would control what I wore, who I had as friends, when I went out, what I should say, believe or do.

My career has never been linear, but I experienced some enormous milestones in the time that I was with him. My confidence had started to grow and James sensed it. He knew he had to manage the situation or risk me recognising my own power.

Like clockwork the constant little digs began: 'Don't give up your day job,' he said. 'Everyone has their five minutes of fame,' he would add, trying to make me feel like a blip and a flash in the pan. I realised in that moment that my empowerment was in direct competition with his ability to feel powerful. For him it had to be one or the other. I saw clearly for the first time how threatened he was by me recognising my own potential. I couldn't grow in his eyes without him shrinking. Everything in our relationship depended on a power dynamic in which I was subservient. And from that moment, it got really bad.

The dramas with James escalated and permeated every part of my life. My friends grew weary of my constantly depleted emotional state. Even my mother reached her limit. Everyone was frustrated by what seemed like my inability to help myself. Narcissists are so very good at convincing you that life without them will be a lonely place. I could see his problems but part of me still felt lucky that this sexy and deceptively charming man cared about me, someone who's been made to feel monstrous her entire life, someone as socially precarious as me. He fed off my desperation.

James controlled my friendships; he was critical of my weight, my appearance and supervised what

I wore. Being very aware that I had to appear as perfect as possible for him to love me, I learned to self-harm in ways that were undetectable. I would cut the soles of my feet and say I'd slipped or stepped on a glass. I'd burn myself 'accidentally' with my hair tongs.

It was only when he started to become radicalised by far-right ideologies and obsessed with online conspiracy theories, that I started to see how he mistreated others – mainly through comments online, although listening to his opinions in-person wasn't great either – and I could begin to separate myself from him. We had a blow-up fight, we broke up, and he disappeared completely, only coming back to collect his things.

When I had my first relationship with a woman, I realised how much my identity and concept of love was dependent on the company and validation of men. I'd never considered myself to be bisexual or pansexual. I knew I was attracted to women but as I was generally more attracted to men, I thought this was a choice I had to make rather than embracing the fluidity of an expansive sexuality.

I felt a deep connection with Ava as soon as I saw her. It was a new feeling but a welcome one. She was incredibly beautiful, French Algerian with dark, sculpted features, olive skin and glossy black hair that skimmed her shoulders. Initially I didn't realise that she was also trans. She had a smile that would say exactly what she was thinking, without even having to say it, and I think that's what I loved most about her, the way she carried her honesty. I wanted to know her better. She had this immense depth to her that drew people in. She kept most of them at arm's length, but never me. I met her when I was DJing in a store opening off Carnaby Street; she had seen my set advertised and wanted to introduce herself. I liked her confidence and suggested that we go for a drink.

When I discovered that she was trans, it gave me pause. I had internalised so much hatred, and after all if I as a trans woman wasn't worthy of love, then why should she be. But it ceased to matter with her. We had a drink and got on instantly, talking about being trans and how awful it is to date straight cisgender men. Once we left the bar we carried on chatting on the Tube and she walked me home under her umbrella, her hand locked with mine. I could tell that this was unlike anything that I'd felt before, that it was more than a friendship. I wanted to kiss her but wasn't sure if I was the only one feeling these feelings. Thankfully I wasn't.

Ava was my first relationship with an equal. It felt like the first time I wasn't being weaponised for someone else's interests, which had been my experience with men up to that point. She was so self-realised; she held a mirror up to me. She held me accountable in ways which were healthy, unlike my previous relationships where I wasn't being held accountable, I was being punished. We dated on and off for three years while my career rose exponentially. It was the first time I'd been loved with passion and respect, the first time I was happy and secure in a relationship.

Unfortunately, I was the saboteur. The relationship ended because I think I couldn't accept that kind of love. I thought love had to be difficult, that it had to be passionate in a way that was quite hurtful. All I'd known in love was to work really hard to win crumbs of it. I didn't know how to reciprocate Ava's love. I think I also experienced an element of internalised homophobia – I struggled to see myself with a woman in the long term. This wasn't something I'd ever imagined myself doing when I was younger. I was panicked at what this meant about my sexuality: what was I now that I was romantically involved with a woman?

My relationship with sex wasn't how it is now. Before Ava, I wasn't participating in sex, I was performing sex. I was engaging in it in a way that involved around the man ejaculating. I was so focused on performing in a way that got them off that I wasn't really enjoying it. Rather than actually connecting with my partner, I was calculating ways to seem desirable, mimicking pornography. Was I arching my back in a way that made my body look sexy, was I moaning in a way that kept him hard, was I encouraging him in a way that made him feel like a big man? With Ava it was just us without any expectation; she thought I was beautiful and I thought she was beautiful, and I found it quite unsettling. I didn't love myself enough then to be loved unconditionally. For the first time, I was quite scared of becoming like my own bad partners, someone who wasn't worthy of Ava's love. Someone who was irresponsible with their partner's joy, trust and commitment. To this day, I feel remorse at how I behaved. All of my other relationships feel like they played out but with Ava I still wonder what might have happened to me if I'd been able to accept her love.

After Ava, I've come to prioritise and value femininity in all the people I've dated, be it women or men. I used to think my role was to be feminine so someone masculine would love me. But now I understand that femininity is just who I am; it can't be manipulated because it is my power. Being with Ava allowed me the experience of an equal form of love that wasn't based on a transaction, a fetish or a projection. It wasn't dependent on me pandering to them to uphold their vision of themselves. That was how I'd always experienced relationships before. It had always been about how I slotted into other people's lives. With Ava I felt seen for the first time, I felt like I had my first truly intimate experience. It was the first time I grew in a relationship rather than just accepting the scraps of romance I'd been offered all those years. Since then, I've met men who have done the work on themselves, who've had conversations and processed their sexuality. Society has changed a great deal and allowed space for people to express themselves and ask questions and not hide from their desires, should they be so inclined. In truth all this could always have existed, but I was not in a position to allow it into my life until I did the work myself.

Doing the work for me was me contextualising my existence, understanding my ancestors – queer ancestors, Black ancestors, trans ancestors – understanding how society has come to this place and how I navigate it. It was about making healthier choices, understanding the role that I play in life. It was about choosing to lead my life from a place of growth and love. We all have a moral compass when it comes to other people, but it becomes blurry and disorientated when we have a lack of self-esteem or self-worth. Why was I putting up with people who treated me in a way I would hate to see a loved one be treated?

The more I saw myself as worthwhile, the less I could accept toxic 'love'; it simply didn't appeal to me. I used to feel very angry at how men have treated me but as I've worked on leaving no part of myself unexamined, I've come to realise that happy and fulfilled people are not cruel to others in this way. Truly happy and fulfilled people are not cruel to themselves in this way either. You cannot love someone fully in their complexity unless you love yourself in your own.

Race

I first heard the words 'Black Lives Matter' in July of 2014, after the video of Eric Garner's death went viral on social media.

His final words, 'I can't breathe', played on a loop in my mind for the days, weeks and months that followed. I found it difficult to concentrate on my work. I became withdrawn, irritable, insular and distracted as I tried to process what I had just witnessed. I could feel anger cramping in my body like a dull tension that I couldn't shake, a weight that was just always there. I wanted to cry it out, but I couldn't. I wanted to understand how this could happen, but I couldn't. I wanted to bury the feelings deep down, just like I always had from the time I was a child, when I'd learned that I wasn't just different but that the nature of my difference posed a potential threat to others. But I couldn't.

When I saw Eric Garner's body lying suffocated by the police, I thought, what if this was my father? What if a video of my father's last moments was being shared on social media? Would this video still be shared with such little thought if Eric was a white man? It was the apathy to Black death that hurt me the most, followed by the learned disregard for Black pain teamed with performative concern.

It was the lack of respect that Black bodies endure, not only in life, but also in death. We don't see videos of dead white people on social media because there is a social value attached to the life of a white person. Black people are not seen in the same way. We are so used to seeing Black bodies enduring violence; we are taught that Black history began with violence; we are taught that Black bodies are violent. So, it has become an ingrained disconnect within us; it is as if the violence is expected, normalised, unsurprising. If you're white you can ignore it. If you're Black you learn to endure it. But it's always there. In the back of your mind, this could be me next.

The years following Eric Garner's death provided little reassurance. On 12 August 2017, the world watched in horror as white supremacists, neo-Nazis, Klansmen, neo-fascists, neo-Confederates, alt-right nationalists and right-wing militia descended on Charlottesville, Virginia's former Lee Park (now Market Street Park), for the Unite the Right rally, organised in protest against the proposed removal of the Confederate statue of slave owner Robert E. Lee.

The captured footage looked like something out of a horror movie, with the attendees carrying lit tiki torches and chanting 'you will not replace us' and 'white lives matter', a realised nightmare for many people of colour who feared that something like this would happen following the inauguration of Donald Trump. The riot culminated in anti-racist protester Heather Heyer being murdered by neo-Nazi James Alex Fields Jr, who deliberately drove his car at speed into a crowd of peaceful protesters, killing her and injuring thirty-five others. He was later sentenced to life in prison in 2019.

Watching the events of the Charlottesville riot unfold felt both unreal and yet anticipated, with racial tensions on both sides of the Atlantic reaching boiling point. Racism wasn't being talked about in the mainstream, at least not from the perspective of people of colour. It was consistently downplayed through an uncritical lens. The idea that white supremacy posed a serious and imminent threat to the public was posed as an abstract concept – often minimised under a shadow of Islamophobia, as if white society couldn't possibly be considered a serious threat to others, *so look over there...* Like many others around the world, I watched in anger and fear. I felt helpless and infuriated that something like this had been able to happen, that the threat that the far right posed to the general public hadn't been anticipated or intercepted. If it had been 400 Muslims or BLM protesters marching with weapons, you know that the National Guard would have been there from the start.

Horrified and alarmed at what I was seeing unfold in real time, I took to social media to vent my anger and frustration with white society's unwillingness to fully grapple with the symptoms of the system it benefits from. I didn't have as big a following as I do now, just around 5,000 followers, most of whom understood the context of what I was speaking about and were equally appalled at what was unfolding. I wanted to express that these people were not merely just a few bad eggs; they were representatives and products of a system of oppression that has power and influence in every pocket of western society – from politics to the police, healthcare, housing, education and employment.

Systemic racism is present in every single governing system that people of colour navigate on a daily basis. It is maintained because it is beneficial to those who hold power, power that has been obtained and is maintained via the forced labour, disenfranchisement, marginalisation and dehumanisation of people of colour. Charlottesville was not and should not be seen as an isolated event. It was an inevitable manifestation of a society unwilling to grapple with the foundations on which it was built.

A switch had been flipped. I wasn't as concerned with the reaction to the post as I was with the reaction to the protest. My focus was not for one minute on what people thought about me addressing something that was now undeniable. I had well and truly run out of fucks to give. White supremacy exists, it poses an immediate and significant threat to society and it has now been televised in real time for all of us to witness. Pulling focus away from the violence of the protest to condemn people of colour instead, for reacting in a way that isn't deemed appropriate in the eyes of white society, indicates a lack of empathy and of understanding of the impact that witnessing instances of racial violence has on people of colour. It shows just how unfamiliar white society is with being critiqued, and how rarely the legacy of whiteness and colonialism is critiqued as a social construct within the mainstream.

Honestly, I don't have energy to talk about the racial violence of white people any more. Yes ALL white people. Because most of ya'll don't even realise or refuse to acknowledge that your existence, privilege and success as a race is built on the backs, blood and death of people of colour. Your entire existence is drenched in racism. From micro-aggressions to terrorism, you built the blueprint for this shit. Come see me when you realise racism isn't learned, it's inherited and consciously or unconsciously passed down through privilege. Once white people begin to admit their race is the most violent and oppressive force of nature on Earth... then we can talk.

At the time of posting, I had minimal negative pushback from my followers. Some people took issue with my tone but after being reminded about what I was reacting to, realised that their focus was on the wrong thing. They realised that expecting people of colour not to be angry or not to express that anger about racial violence and the legacy of white supremacy is what allows such violence to go unchecked. When we don't acknowledge the source of the violence, how do we have a hope of changing the trajectory? I wanted to say, very candidly, that all of white society plays a role within white supremacy, whether it be passive or active, unless they are actively working to become anti-racist and consciously striving to unpack their relationship with the social construct that is 'whiteness'.

The main issue that the post came up against is that many, if not most, white people do not think of themselves as a particular ethnicity because until very recently, they haven't had to think about it or address the way that their race interacts with the rest of the world as a whole.

The way that white history is taught from a very early age is not accurate. It is seen through a very narrow lens that minimises, if not completely erases, much of the harm that the concept of white western ideals has had across the globe. We are not taught an accurate account of how a little European island managed to make itself so rich; we are not taught about the exploitation, enslavement and abuse that made that possible and still makes it possible today. Racism was spoken about in a way that lacked nuance, divorced from the everyday lived experiences of people of colour living within a system built on white supremacy. Instead, racism was democratised as individual instances of prejudice that affect all people, regardless of whether they are Black, white, Asian or indigenous. In reality, white people do not experience systemic racism; they are the beneficiaries of the system, with factors of class, sexuality, nationality, gender and ability playing a role in their proximity to its power. White supremacy is inherited though a culture of indoctrination, where whiteness is presented as the pinnacle; its global impact erased, criticism suppressed, resistance demonised and status quo maintained.

★

On 6 February 2017 I received an email from the biggest beauty brand in the world, L'Oréal, with a request to be part of their new True Match foundation campaign due to launch later that year. I had to read the email at least four times, scanning the sender's address and the offer to make absolutely sure it was real. I was in complete disbelief, I couldn't believe that such an influential industry giant wanted to work with someone like me... Trying not to get too excited, as I was sure there was a catch, I accepted. I thought, it must just be something small, but it was L'Oréal, so it was big for me regardless.

We shot the campaign the following month in Paris. While sitting on the Eurostar it struck me that I'd never seen a transgender model work with L'Oréal in a campaign before. I put it out of my mind that I could possibly be the first – that couldn't possibly happen to someone like me who until now only had one major brand campaign under their belt. But later that day it was confirmed to me that I was indeed the first, it was due to be a big moment and I should prepare for everything being about to change.

Five months passed before the campaign launched on Sunday 27 August 2017. I was working at a bar in Brixton at the time to supplement my income from modelling. I'd decided to stop working in clubs and focus all my energy into building my name within the fashion and beauty industries, hustling to get my career into a healthy place for when the campaign launched. Nightlife had started to feel repetitive; I'd had a good run but now was the time for me to focus on what I truly wanted for my future and that wasn't the London party-girl life that I had lived for the past seven years. I'd had fun, I'd grown up and learnt a lot of valuable lessons along the way, but it was time to move up from that life, even if that meant getting a part-time job to facilitate the transition.

In the time between shooting the True Match campaign and the launch, I had shot two other beauty campaigns that were due to be released later that year, one for a skincare brand and another for a perfume. I felt proud of myself for the changes that I had made to my life and was excited to see the hard work and sacrifice beginning to pay off.

The campaign launched in a big way. Suddenly I was being interviewed by major fashion publications such as British *Vogue* and *Elle*. The news that L'Oréal had hired their first transgender model spread faster than I had anticipated, or rather than I had dared to dream. I made the news across the world, and my social media presence began to rise, with hundreds of new followers every minute. I couldn't believe that I was in this position, able to represent my community in such a big way. I wanted to use this as an opportunity to bring conversations I had been having in activist spaces into the mainstream. It was a lot to process. I finally let myself begin to feel excited about being part of the project. I guess part of me didn't want to fully believe it until I could see it in front of my eyes, until it was really real. But I had absolutely no idea just how real things were about to get.

My post in response to the Charlottesville riot had been screenshot and sent to the *Daily Mail* by somebody I went to university with. We never saw eye to eye and I had previously publicly called them out for sharing a meme of Michelle Obama's face next to an image of a cast member from the movie *Planet of the Apes*. On 31 August I received a call from L'Oréal while out shopping in Soho for an event I had been invited to that evening. They told me that the *Daily Mail* had contacted them to make them aware that they were publishing a story regarding a 'racist post' that one of their models had published on social media.

My heart immediately sank. Even though I knew what I had written wasn't wrong, I also knew how it would be spun, especially as it was the *Daily Mail* spinning it. L'Oréal advised me to go home immediately, not to post anything to social media and not to attend the event that evening. They said that I should lie low and stay by my phone until the article had been published so that their crisis team could advise on the next steps. I tried to explain myself to them, clarifying that it was a post in response to the Charlottesville disaster, I tried to get them to understand what I meant by the post, why I posted it and that it wasn't something I had posted since the campaign launch, but after reading the headline, their response was that as a brand they couldn't stand by the racial statements I had made. My contract was terminated and I was publicly sacked.

The article dropped that evening at 11.01pm. It immediately blew up and spread across social media like wildfire. The headline read: 'L'Oreal's first transgender model is SACKED by cosmetics giant after claiming "ALL white people" are racist in extraordinary Facebook rant'. Within a few days it had made worldwide news channels, and it was in pretty much every single mainstream newspaper and online media outlet in the UK and America. There was no preparing for this. I felt cold and numb. I couldn't do much but crawl into a ball at the foot of my bed and stare at the wall, bleary-eyed, as tears ran down my face. I didn't know what to do. I had no manager to advise me, no publicist to change the narrative, no access to significant funds for a lawyer. I let it all wash over me for a day. Then I decided to fight back.

My email inbox was full of interview requests from every major news network in the UK. I knew that my only shot – if not at redemption, then at least at damage limitation – was to take advantage of every single opportunity to speak my truth, to offer context to the article that created a completely false image of who I was as a human being.

The conservative press was having a field day, labelling me a racist for daring to point out that racism exists and that it benefits white people. Social media abuse was like nothing I've ever seen. I was receiving death threats, rape threats, with faceless user profiles telling me that they knew where I lived and were watching me, that they wanted to decapitate me and 'fuck my skull'. I was afraid to leave the house, looking over my shoulder at every turn.

From *Channel 4 News* to *Good Morning Britain*, to *BBC News*, *ITV News*, *Sky News* – I took every single opportunity to tell my side of the story. I didn't know how people were going to take it, but at this point I really didn't have anything to lose. Every single brand partnership that I had developed was now off the table. The campaigns that I had shot before the L'Oréal launch were shelved. I had just about enough money to feed myself and pay my rent. I had *absolutely nothing* to lose.

*

In the dark place where I'd found myself in the days following the L'Oréal scandal, I felt a sense of helplessness not unlike that of my schooldays. Sprawled eventually at rock bottom, I realised I had two choices. I could destroy myself and let the world watch, or I could start to figure myself out in the way that critical race theory had helped me question society. After all, society had made me too. Homophobia and racism aren't rooted in fact. They're beliefs that you can pull apart, then you're left with your own pain. I looked at all the ugly parts of my character, and saw all the hatred I'd aimed at myself. I was behaving in the way that other people often treated me. I started questioning why I hated myself. I was killing myself for other people and I didn't want to give them that pleasure.

The one bright spark in this dark time was that my relationship with my family had started to heal. My mum hadn't spoken to me for a year and a half after I'd come out to her as trans. I'd stopped going home or making any contact with them, leading me to seek yet more attention from my abusive partner – who was thrilled. It was ironically my father who got my mum and me to talk to each other; he rebuilt the family in a way that meant we now saw each other as adults rather than me being the perennially disappointing child. It's not something I'd ever have imagined after my childhood with him. I still had a lot of resentment towards him, but he got my mum and me in a room together. He knew I needed family and that if we didn't reconnect, they would completely lose me, and I would completely lose myself.

When we met, we all realised that for us to be a family, we *all* had to transition in one way or another. I had to start acknowledging that my parents were human beings who made mistakes, who acted out of a lack of understanding of their own emotions. Before this, I'd really just thought of them as people who'd made me but couldn't accept me. I hadn't considered that they might be people with their own traumas and their own wounds. I learned to see their conflict through a different lens and extend forgiveness to myself but also to them. I could see how my father, a man of few words, felt tremendous guilt at the way my childhood had gone and remorse for the way he had acted. You can't change the past, but you can begin anew when you agree to start with a foundation of mutual respect. We're now building a relationship on the basis of understanding that the past was painful but the future is ours to shape in a healthy and happy way.

I remember feeling anxious at the time because we'd only just sorted everything out when the L'Oréal controversy blew up. My mum was initially confused by what I'd posted – she asked me if I thought she was violent because she was white. I could see how she might think that, given the way the media had deliberately framed my words. When I explained what I'd said in context, she understood immediately. The family then became a resource for me during the fallout. My father and I started having conversations about race and he opened up about his experiences of racism. It was a connection I'd always wanted to have with my father, to share our experience of Blackness, and that intimacy was the best thing to come out of all of this.

The tide began to turn after my appearance on *Good Morning Britain*, which, despite being one of the most anxiety-inducing fifteen minutes of my life, served to prove my point. Sitting opposite presenters Piers Morgan and Susanna Reid, I found myself in the position of being shouted at by a fifty-year-old cis white guy with an axe to grind at 7am on national television. I stood my ground, and I let him shout until he was quite literally red in the face, knowing that every time he shouted over me, denying the existence of racism in the UK, he was only proving my point. The appearance went viral, globally, sparking a debate on racism in the UK, and on white supremacy and how we speak about it on both sides of the Atlantic. The tide was beginning to turn. People were beginning to understand the context behind what I was saying. They understood that I hadn't just taken to social media in an 'extraordinary rant'; I was critiquing the system that we all need to live within and being reprimanded for doing so.

Looking back at it, I suppose I shouldn't have been too surprised by the public reaction – the post was blunt and angry but it wasn't untrue. Things have changed rapidly since then but at the time that post left me out in the cold. Though it was only six years ago, models were not encouraged then to say anything that might be deemed unpopular or divisive, regardless of whether what they were saying was in fact correct. Now, being socially conscious is en vogue. Black Lives Matter caused a major cultural shift, and before that there was #metoo. In this cultural moment, authenticity stands for something and brands have picked up on this public shift. Today you'll see Gigi and Bella Hadid using their voices to educate their followers on the war on Palestine and keeping their jobs; Cara Delevingne is out and proud, representing the LGBTQ community and still working hard; and Naomi Campbell is more forthright about racism than she ever has been in the past and is still as much in demand as she has ever been.

I feel like my experience being sacked by L'Oréal and the debacle that followed helped to play a part in that shift within the industry between brands and models. In the three years that followed, I continued to speak up about transphobia and racism within the UK. I worked with charities such as Stonewall, UK Black Pride and Mermaids. In 2018 *Cosmopolitan* UK presented me with their Disruptor/Changemaker of the Year award. The following year, I was appointed as a UN Women UK Changemaker, given an honorary doctorate for my contribution in campaigning for transgender rights from the University of Brighton and announced as Campaigner of the Year at the British LGBT Awards. Despite it being an extremely challenging time, to say the very least, and perhaps ageing me a good few years, I have absolutely no regrets. None.

Like many Black British people of my generation, I felt systemic racism first creep into my consciousness following the murder of Stephen Lawrence in 1993. Stephen, who was eighteen years old at the time, was waiting at a bus stop in south-east London, when he was murdered in a racially motivated attack. Five suspects were arrested, but not charged, which subsequently led to revelations following an inquiry headed by Sir William Macpherson, which found that the original investigation into Stephen's murder had itself been impacted by racism within the police force and Crown Prosecution Service. Macpherson concluded that Stephen had been killed because he was Black and that the Metropolitan Police Service was institutionally racist itself. I remember that the story of Stephen Lawrence's murder was unavoidable: it was everywhere, everyone was talking about it, on every front page, on every news station of every channel. I remember noticing how different the conversations were with the Black side of my family in Wembley from those with the white people that surrounded me where I grew up in Essex.

The white people around me in 1999, when I was twelve, seemed to recoil when the subject of institutional racism came up in the publishing of the Macpherson Report. I clearly remember them talking about how a few bad apples shouldn't be indicative of the police as a whole, that it was unfair and counterproductive to paint all police with the same brush, that not all police are racist and that the word racism shouldn't be thrown around. The consensus was that the police were there to keep us safe and we should support them. Time after time the conversation was shut down and squashed once the word racism came up.

But the conversations that I had in Wembley when staying with my auntie, uncle and cousins were very different. There was a clear sense of urgency to the situation, as if it had happened to a member of our family, as if it still could happen to a member of our family. I could sense that the violence towards us was just as much within the police as it was in the streets, if not more so. That we weren't safe from the police and they should be held accountable for their actions. In those moments I became more and more aware of the duality of my racial heritage, and realised that Black and white people navigate very different existences. I was left unsure where to place myself, unsure of where I fitted in, or if there was even room for me in these discussions.

We do not talk about race here.
We do not make things about race here.

Don't play the race card.

YOU don't get to play the victim here.

Growing into my teens, I started spending less time in Wembley so I could focus on my studies. This meant that my access to Blackness and Black people all but disappeared. With no smartphone, no social media and no other Black people in my school, I struggled to find role models to look up to, or anyone who could help me understand what it meant to be Black, or mixed race. I had no sounding board or support network when it came to understanding the subject of race. I always knew race mattered, but where I lived, it was thought a non-issue; racism was considered to be a thing of the past. At this point in time, I was being bullied quite relentlessly, mostly with regard to my sexuality and feminine mannerisms, but I was also experiencing a constant stream of racial micro-aggressions from my classmates and some members of staff at my school.

However, talking about race and racism was considered as bad if not worse than actually being racist or holding racist views. The term racism where I grew up was reserved for cross-burning, KKK hood-wearing neo-Nazis with DIY swastika tattoos and Southern American rednecks. There was no notion that it could be expressed more subtly than that. The idea that it might be systemic and built into the structure of society was unthinkable. Racism was not a word that you could use freely without being confronted as if you were yourself the perpetrator. For most of the white people I grew up around, it was something done by *other people*. And yet, I kept experiencing it.

There's only so many times you can hear 'go back to where you came from', or 'if you don't like it here, leave', before you start to feel like an unwanted guest on your own doorstep. There's only so many times you can be told by white classmates that their parents 'don't like Black people, but you're OK', that 'I wouldn't date a Black person, but I don't see you as Black', that 'you're not like other Black people', before you start to detach from your own Blackness. Not only do you start to feel that you're not welcome, but you start to believe and accept it yourself.

That was before I had learned that racism isn't an accident, that it isn't some inconvenient and miraculous stain on society; it is an intentional system of marginalisation built into the foundation of society as we know it. Going by what you're taught in school, it's an unfortunate flaw in an otherwise benign, egalitarian social structure. But hopefully, we are transitioning into a society which has more conversations now about how this is far from the truth.

As just one example of how the truth can be obscured: in the first half of the nineteenth century, the craniologist Samuel Morton was one of America's most highly respected scientists and his many accolades included President of the Academy of Natural Sciences. Morton had a theory that human intelligence could be categorised by skull size, as the skull determined the size of the brain, and this in turn determined how advanced the person was. He called this theory 'phrenology'. Morton collected about 900 human skulls from around the world, often scavenged from dead soldiers on battlefields and the dead bodies of convicts, filling them with white pepper seeds, and later in his studies, with lead shot to establish their volume. He concluded that humanity could be divided into five separate races and that each of these races was independently created. With no notion of the possibility of bias, subconscious or otherwise, Morton claimed that his findings proved that Caucasians/whites were the most intelligent of the five races, followed by East Asians. Next up were South-East Asians, then Native Americans, and lastly, Africans.

Morton's pseudoscientific methodology was held in high regard and not questioned because his work upheld the status quo. It provided a patina of legitimacy and an alleged 'scientific' defence to the exertion of white supremacy, to racial segregation, racial slavery and the belief that Black people were an inferior species. He was, as you can imagine, a particular favourite of the American Southern states.

Morton's work can be traced back as one of the first instances of scientific racism, a dangerous social building block in the evolution of systemic and notably, medical racism. But the idea of the white race as supreme didn't start with Morton, and neither did the idea of the human race existing as several separate entities.

The term 'Caucasian' was first coined in Germany in 1780. Still widely used today, it was born out of an ideology entwined with scientific and religious racism. Following a visit to the Caucasus Mountains, situated at the intersection of Europe and Asia, German anthropologist Johann Friedrich Blumenbach was so taken aback by the beauty of the region that he decided to name what has come to be known as the white race after it, even though the Caucasus region is actually home to a wide array of ethnic groups. Blumenbach believed that the white race was closest to godliness and proceeded to name four other races that he considered to be 'physically and morally "degenerate" forms of "God's original creation"'. Africans, excluding North Africans, who were included within the Caucasian ideology, were identified as 'Ethiopians' or 'Black'. Native Americans were identified as 'Red'. Asians who weren't considered to be Caucasian were divided into two separate races, with Japanese and Chinese people being identified as 'Mongolian' or 'Yellow' and Pacific

Islanders and Aboriginal Australians being classified as 'Malayan' or 'Brown'.

While science has long disabused these notions, the concept of race continues to hold a tight grasp on the world. Hundreds of years have passed in which the ideology of the white race as superior has been woven into the fabric of society in such a way that, while it may not be acceptable to express the opinion as starkly as before, it is for much of western society an accepted norm.

Systemic racism is the lasting legacy of intentional acts of mass oppression, population suppression, disenfranchisement and the hoarding of wealth, power and resources based on race. It is insidious in nature; it impacts everything from our criminal justice system to our healthcare, to the police, to beauty standards, to the workplace and employment, to the education system, to housing and politics. I'd grown up being taught that Malcolm X was a terrorist, that he was too radical. It was while watching a video of his on YouTube on the functioning of the police that I first realised that oppression has been carefully curated and planned. Malcolm X had become a social pariah for being the wrong type of activist in the eyes of white society. A neutered version of Martin Luther King's legacy – one in which all he did was preach non-violence – was considered the right type of activism. My politics were more in line with those of Malcolm X.

It's racial oppression that has become embedded within our social systems and has often come to be accepted as the norm. It's a term that has evolved from 'institutional racism', which was first coined in 1967 by US civil rights activist Kwame Ture and political scientist Charles V. Hamilton. In their book *Black Power:The Politics of Liberation,*Ture and Hamilton discuss the difference between individual instances of racism, which are often overt, and racism that exists as part of a system, which is often covert, and less recognisable should you be white yourself. Ture and Hamilton state that institutional racism 'exists in the operation of established and respected forces in the society, and thus receives far less public condemnation than individual racism'. While the functioning of systemic racism may be less conspicuous than individualised racism, it is just as dangerous, if not more so.

Black History Month was first celebrated in the UK in 1987, organised by Ghanaian-born Akyaaba Addai-Sebo, who said he kickstarted the event as a response to seeing Black children in Britain disconnecting from their African roots. My school's version of Black History Month was wheeling a TV out from the stock cupboard to play thirty or forty minutes-worth of *Amistad* or *The Color Purple* on VHS, while the whole class took turns at looking at me every time the words Black, nigger or negro were mentioned. I wanted to run away as far as I could in those moments, not because I didn't want to learn, but because I knew that outside of the faux interest in Black History Month, I wasn't allowed to speak about the reality of my Black present, any month.

As important as Black history is, we need to be able to speak about what it means to be Black in today's society, and how it feels. The only way we can do this is if the collective lived experiences of Black people are listened to and taken on board as fact, not dismissed as opinion. We need to move past the idea that systemic racism is a matter of perception and understand that it is the objective product of deliberate actions intended to target and oppress people of colour.

We need to transition away from the tired and inaccurate idea that Black history started with slavery, that Black contributions are only worth mentioning when they exist within a proximity to whiteness, when they are measured against whiteness or within white systems. The way in which I was taught about history was almost solely through a cisgender, straight, white male lens, which sent a message that people like me simply didn't exist within British history, that we had achieved nothing worthy of note, upholding the idea that this country isn't really mine to take advantage of at the end of my school experience.

Not only this, but what kind of message does non-inclusive teaching send to white students? If white faces are the only faces that they see when learning about historic achievements, then whiteness becomes synonymous with greatness and the foundation for their unconscious bias begins to solidify. I wish I had learned about the Kingdom of Aksum when I was at school; I wish I had learned about the Mali and Benin empires, just as I learned about the Roman and British empires. I wish I hadn't been given the impression that Africa was a barren wasteland. I wish I knew what colonial riches looked like in their own countries.

After numerous physical and verbal fights at school stemming from being called racist names, I was suspended twice and threatened with expulsion. I became one of the children Akyaaba was speaking about, numb to my Blackness and numb to myself, not because I wanted to be white, but because I was tired of fighting a hopeless battle, blind, with no allies.

Despite still holding within me a massive amount of internalised racism that would often reveal itself in saying tone-deaf and uneducated things, I had started developing a more critical, analytical gaze towards race at university. I attended ACAS (African, Caribbean and Asian Society) meetings on the Sussex University campus with some friends who were studying there. There wasn't that much diversity on my campus so I sneaked in with them and sat at the back. Being there and listening to attendees share their experiences made me realise how much

I had been repressing my own. I found out how little I knew about Black history, and about the US civil rights movement beyond the whitewashed image of Dr Martin Luther King. I discovered an affinity with the words of Malcolm X, someone who until then I had been led to believe was a divisive figure without warrant. My eyes were beginning to open; I was beginning to see how deeply the racism I experienced in my childhood had permeated my consciousness. So deep that I didn't even see myself for who I truly was.

Learning about the US civil rights movement through a Black lens, rather than just relying on what I was taught as part of a syllabus built for white pupils by a white education board, was crucial in enabling me to look at how race functions within society in a critical way. It encouraged me to look deeper, to seek the information out through reading about critical race theory. It began to pull together so many threads. It didn't just stop at race. Once you start looking at underlying structures, the sand shifts beneath your feet. I realised that my idea of feminism comprised women who were themselves exploitative and privileged – women who behaved like white men. I started grappling with the functioning of class within society. I began examining the language that I used and started recognising offensive terms that had unwittingly made their way into my vocabulary. I started examining my attractions, my interests, my friendships, my reactions, where I got my news and where I spent my money.

If I have one crucial piece of advice that will stand you well in any moment of transition in your life, it is that instead of waiting for the information to come to you, go to it. Question why things exist. Only then will you see how much of history is whitewashed, watered down and appropriated to centre western European narratives of triumph. If I had taken the initiative to seek out information about the LGBT rights movement, I would have found that it was a Black trans woman, Marsha P. Johnson, a Latinx trans woman, Sylvia Rivera, and a butch lesbian, Stormé DeLarverie, who were the catalysts of the 1969 Stonewall Riots in New York City, which led to the first ever Pride march, which birthed the Gay Rights Movement, which became the LGBT movement. But I didn't, largely because I assumed that, much like the majority of the history that we are taught in the British academic syllabus, it was cisgender, white, gay men that initiated that movement.

Following the resurgence of the Black Lives Matter movement in response to the murder of George Floyd, who was killed while under arrest on 25 May 2020, I found myself contextualising the movement on social media and talking about the historical factors behind it. White people who hadn't directly been affected by racism were beginning to see how it was for the rest of us, and they were beginning to piece the puzzle together. Some companies wanted to change their working practices in earnest, and some knew they had to make changes for the optics. Either way, more and more brands started wanting to be part of the conversation, if not the solution. They started looking towards their companies as microcosms of our flawed world and to hiring more marginalised employees, both behind the scenes and in front of the camera. Many FTSE 100 companies, social media companies, fashion brands and councils began asking me to consult for them. I had come in from the cold.

On 2 June 2020, a collective action called Blackout Tuesday swept across social media, to protest against systemic racism. It was originally organised within the music industry to show solidarity following the murders of George Floyd, Ahmaud Arbery and Breonna Taylor. Black squares began being shared on social media far and wide, with many non-music-related public figures, brands and companies sharing the squares too. Although it was well intentioned, many Black social media users were quick to question how effective or necessary the simple sharing of a black square on social media really was, in challenging the deeply ingrained systemic racism within our society, and affirmed that what we need to see is a tangible commitment to change.

To me it gave a feeling resonant of the 'hopes and prayers' responses seen after every American school shooting. Hopes and prayers don't change anything, neither does the image of a black square. We are way past the point of identifying that the issue exists; what we need is critical accountability with tangible commitments to reform.

★

Scrolling through Instagram I landed on a grid post from L'Oréal in which a black square was shared along with the caption 'Speaking up is always worth it'. When I read that I almost fell out of my chair. I couldn't believe that after all of that public furore and shaming that I experienced in response to my contract being terminated, for saying what everybody was now saying on social media, this is where we were. If they had reached out to apologise for everything that sacking me had put me through before they posted that message, then I maybe would have understood, and that's what hurt. It felt entirely performative; it made me feel like I was invisible, that what happened to me as a result of them being unwilling to stand up against racism, didn't matter. Here is my response:

I wanted to give L'Oréal 48 hours before writing this to see if a public apology was possible. But their choice to ignore me and not acknowledge the emotional, mental and professional harm that they caused me since sacking me in 2017, after speaking out about white supremacy and racism, speaks volumes.

So does their choice to not engage with the thousands of Black community members and allies who have left comments of concern on their last two posts, in response to their claim to support the Black community, despite an evident history of being unwilling to talk about the issues that Black people face globally because of white supremacy.

Black Lives Matter is a movement for the people, by the people. It is not here to be co-opted for capital gain by companies who have no intention of actually having difficult conversations regarding white supremacy, police brutality, colonialism and systemic racism. It cannot be reduced to a series of corporate trends by brands like L'Oréal who have no intention of actually doing the work to better themselves or taking ownership of their past mistakes or conscious acts of racial bias. I would not have been sacked if I had said what I said and was a cisgender, straight, white woman. It just wouldn't have happened. If you want to stand with Black Lives Matter then get your own house in order first.

This could have been a moment of redemption for L'Oréal, a chance for them to make amends and lead by example. We all get things wrong, we all make mistakes, but it's where you go from there that is a signifier of who you are. L'Oréal claiming to stand with the Black community, yet also refusing to engage with the community on this issue, or apologise for the harm they caused to a Black female queer transgender employee, shows us who they are – just another big brand who seeks to capitalise from a marginalised movement, by widening their audience and attempting to improve their public image. Brands need to be aware of their own track record. It's unacceptable to claim to stand with us, if the receipts show a history of silencing Black voices.

Speaking out can't only be 'worth it' when you're white. Black voices matter.

The post went viral, with social media users putting pressure on L'Oréal to acknowledge their mistake – not for standing up against racism, but for sacking one of their employees for speaking up against racism when it wasn't commercially beneficial to do so. All I wanted was an apology, an acknowledgement that they got it wrong.

A week passed without contact or comment and a friend of mine, actress Jameela Jamil, reached out to see if I was doing OK. I was feeling pretty low by that point, almost gaslit. Seeing that post, and the complete disregard for when I spoke up, made me relive a lot of the hurt and sadness of 2017. A few days later she called me to let me know that she had reached out to L'Oréal to tell them her thoughts on the situation and was working to help facilitate a reconciliation between us. At this point I really didn't want to reconcile: I was angry, I wanted answers, I wanted an apology.

Two weeks had passed since Blackout Tuesday and Jameela told me that she had spoken to L'Oréal, who had asked if I would be willing to have a Zoom meeting with Delphine Viguier-Hovasse, Head of L'Oréal, to try and resolve this seemingly endless saga. At first, I was apprehensive. I wanted an apology but I wasn't sure how I felt about having a meeting with them. I wasn't sure what to say, where to even start? I took the day to think and then decided that I would accept their offer.

The meeting was a little tense, yet productive. We spoke at length for little over three hours about the events of 2017 and the years that followed, about where the brand is now under its new leadership and how they plan to enact change moving forward. I got to talk to them directly about how being sacked in such a public manner had an extremely detrimental impact on both my personal and professional life and how I felt they could improve when it came to their impact as a brand. The meeting resulted in a formal acknowledgement and I was asked if I would be interested in rejoining the company to sit on their Diversity, Equity and Inclusion board, which I accepted. As an individual I was hurt, but as an activist it was an opportunity to practise what I preach and make changes within the industry. What better opportunity than to help advise a brand which had previously got it wrong, from the perspective of the person who it had so badly impacted? Following the appointment, I was presented with *Attitude* magazine's Hero of the Year Award, presented by the Editor-in-Chief of British *Vogue*, Edward Enninful. *Glamour* magazine chose me as their Woman of the Year and I did shoots for the covers of *TIME* and *Teen Vogue*, speaking about the importance of progress within the fashion industry and beyond, how change cannot happen with lip service, only with action and resolve.

★

I want to stress that if you don't see your stories being told, then search for them, they are out there and I promise you that it will allow you to feel much less isolated. You don't have to keep escaping when you realise that you belonged all along, you were never an outsider. When it comes to racism our experiences are universal, and sometimes it just requires a bit more diligence and attention to uncover them. Information allows us to transition out of isolation and into community. Information allows us to gain context for why things are how they are, allowing us to bring about real change.

It is widely understood that in order to heal from racial trauma we must address the past, make peace with it and develop a framework that allows us to deal with how it has altered our reality. The same could be said for taking pride in ourselves and thereby giving ourselves value. It is an opportunity for us to collectively heal social trauma in a sustainable way, by addressing where we have come from and what we have been through, and educating wider society to ensure that our experiences aren't repeated. The goal for all of us, regardless of age, is to let go of the shame we hold with regard to who we are and what we are. The shame that in many ways we were taught to hold on to during the formative years of our adolescence. The shame that is passed on through generations because we don't question it – because we're afraid of getting uncomfortable. The goal is to collectively transition out of shame and into pride as a society.

Purpose

I think of my ability to speak and to believe in the position I hold as a snowball. It wasn't as if my candour suddenly sprang from nowhere when I received a platform. No – in childhood the ball started rolling down the hill and by the time I became a public figure, it was big. While the aftermath of being fired by L'Oréal was challenging, I had chosen to make a life for myself based on my values, based on truth and fearlessness, absent of shame. I was going to be myself and not who other people wanted me to be. Among the various challenges and humiliations of being fired from L'Oréal, I was at least spared the agony of second-guessing my position. Ultimately, being vocally myself paid off. I managed to gain success based on authenticity, something that cannot be controlled and therefore limited by other people. I might well have made as much money by conforming, but I wouldn't be me in the same way.

When I first grew interested in activism in my early twenties, my approach was admittedly quite righteous. Not because I thought that I was better than anyone else, but because I was deeply, deeply frustrated. For so long I hadn't been able to put words to how I was feeling or pinpoint the wider context of my past and present experiences. My newly gained insight and perspective felt urgent, and I wanted other people to know what I knew, to see what I saw, to feel how I felt. But like my own journey into understanding the way that oppressive social systems work and the role that we all play within them, other people cannot be forced to understand just because you will them to. We all have a transitional journey of self-reckoning that needs to take place in order for often existential perspectives to be truly taken on board.

When it comes making change within society, a significant hurdle that we face is that every one of us as humans possesses a part of our identity that has the potential to oppress or disenfranchise someone else. The greater the social privilege, the greater the likelihood that the role it plays within our identity and the way that we interact with others and move through the world have been normalised. The vast majority of us, especially those who live in the western world, possess some form of privilege that when acknowledged and unpacked can be harnessed in a way to enact social change, whether that be our class, race, gender identity, sexuality, bodily ability or access. We can only become true allies to each other when we are willing to acknowledge the privilege that we move through the world with and the potential that it holds to do harm to others or to allow harm to continue.

*

My early activism was the manifestation of trying to heal unprocessed trauma aloud. I wanted to be able to turn that trauma and frustration into something tangible that people could see and hear, to ignite empathy, context and understanding, something that would stop the same thing from happening to other people. At the time it felt like I just about had my head above the water, with my toes barely touching the bottom, hoping that in yelling about these injustices, people would jump in and save me and anyone else, everyone else who was feeling the same way or experiencing the same things. But yelling about an issue is only one piece of the puzzle. Without a focus on solutions, without strategy and mobilisation, our yells become background noise, are tuned out, people become numb to them and normality takes on a new form with our pain added to the soundtrack.

Before I discovered intersectional feminism and the work of Professor Kimberlé Williams Crenshaw, many feminist communities that I explored didn't feel like they were something that I as a Black trans woman could relate to. I understood the importance of them,

I knew that they mattered and I was on board, but they didn't feel inclusive of my personal narrative or the needs of my direct communities. It felt like I was taking up space that wasn't mine to stand in, unsure whether the liberation being spoken of had room for me too, unsure whether it recognised my struggle as a woman who was assigned male at birth.

So many of the famous feminist voices that I had grown up knowing spoke largely to the experiences of cisgender white women, often centred around birth rights, experiences that are of course important, but with so little visibility of Black feminist voices, of transgender feminist voices, I felt that maybe the movement didn't have room for me because it wasn't for me. I had to look harder for the perspectives where inclusion was prioritised, where womanhood wasn't spoken about as a monolithic bodily experience, where the difference of our lived experiences as women navigating a patriarchal society were not only acknowledged, but critiqued with an inclusive view of liberation and societal reform.

It was in my mid-twenties that the works of Maya Angelou, bell hooks and Angela Davis transcended from words on a page and became coveted guides to questions and feelings that I had been having my entire life. Discovering Black feminist thought that acknowledged, critiqued and interacted with aspects of social difference as a priority, rather than as an afterthought, made me feel seen and included within the feminist movement. It felt like I was waking up from a life lived on autopilot, experiencing sisterhood from the sidelines. It felt like I was finally paying witness not only to proof that my experiences mattered, were valid and understood, but that my feelings were also vastly shared and connected with others across the world. Reading Maya, bell and Angela helped me to seek out and form connections with cisgender women who held an inclusive understanding of feminism. I no longer felt like an outsider or apologetic for my transness while in women-only spaces. Knowing that my unease with much of second-wave feminism was shared by many of my cisgender peers felt like it was a journey of discovery that we could embark on together, acknowledging each other's individual struggles along the way, but pushing forward as a united sisterhood towards a shared vision of progress.

In 2014 I decided to take my activism offline and started getting more involved in panel talks, safe spaces and meet-ups. It felt affirming to connect in person with people who I had made online connections with and to meet new friends too. Public speaking terrified me, often to the point where I would lose my train of thought, forget the question I was asked or struggle to get my words out whilst breaking out in a cold sweat. Initially, after every panel or speaking engagement, I felt like giving up; I felt that maybe I was more of a writer than a speaker, that I was way out of my depth, but I stuck with it. I was determined to overcome the nerves and work on how I was presenting my ideas and the structure of my arguments. A great deal of it boiled down to confidence, confidence that came with the conviction that can only really arise from standing firm in what you are saying, not just because you believe it or have heard it being said elsewhere, but because you have researched the subject widely, taken on board multiple perspectives, observed the critique from the opposition and formed your own conclusions.

What I enjoyed most about it was plugging into and drawing strength from my community and being able to give strength and perspective to others who were finding their voice too. I often wish that I'd found spaces like that sooner, that maybe many of my escapist tendencies that would often result in self-destructive behaviours were because I was often in environments where my participation and acceptance from others was conditional. In these new spaces the parts of me that I was encouraged to hide, whitewash or not speak about, were acknowledged. I was able to sit and heal, instead of escape and remain numb.

Later that year I joined a feminist collective called Pxssy Palace through Nadine, a friend I met in 2011 while working at Madame JoJo's. We hadn't hung out much since then but after seeing some of my more political posts on social media, they asked me if I would be interested in joining a private Facebook group called 'Racial Black & Brown Hotties', where like-minded queer people of colour could share resources and perspectives on critical race theory, as well as our lived experiences, and connect with each other without being bothered by trolls. After getting to know each other better in the group, they spoke to me about their plans to put together a safe-space club night celebrating Black and indigenous people, and people of colour who are women, queer, intersex, trans or non-binary, who wanted to experience nightlife away from the gaze and often the objectification of cisgender male partygoers. The night had a strict zero-tolerance policy against racism, body shaming, transphobia, homophobia, ableism and classism. After my experiences of having to bite my tongue, code switch and self-censor at many of the nights that I was working, I jumped at the chance when asked to be involved.

Pxssy Palace was more than just a club night. It was a door to the sisterhood I desperately needed. There were seven of us to begin with: Nadine, Skye, Kesang, Sophie, Bemi, Alexa and myself. It was the first time in my life that I was part of a friendship group with cisgender girls and femmes who truly saw me as their equal, who were vocal about and educated on my experience as a transgender woman. I realised how much I had been needing that kind of energy, that kind of platonic feminine intimacy. It went way beyond the validation and tolerance that I had previously accepted – this was an experience of genuine connection, acceptance and mutual respect.

Prior to joining PP I had been starting to build a name for myself in the media, landing a double-page-spread interview in the *Evening Standard*, which led to a short globally aired documentary with CNN and a feature in *Marie Claire*. My career was starting to pick up pace following my campaign with Uniqlo. I began to push myself out of my comfort zone, accepting invitations to speak to bigger crowds with mainstream publications like the *Guardian* and *Huffington Post*. Taking this on felt easier with the support of my girls; it felt less like I was in it alone. Finally, I had friendships with other women who would support and uplift me, who would hold me accountable when I was wrong, who would push me to be my best self, to be bold in how I moved through spaces, to be confident and unapologetic in bringing my whole self to the table. If it wasn't for the bond that I formed with my community and the Pxssy Palace collective, I would have found it so much harder to navigate the years that lay ahead.

★

Following the fallout from the L'Oréal scandal in 2017 and 2018, everything changed. I was now on the front cover of newspapers and magazines across the world, saturating newsfeeds, being spoken about across social media by complete strangers, recognised in the street and debated about on the news. My whole life changed in what felt like the blink of an eye. Suddenly I was navigating an existence that was either seen as polarising and divisive or game-changing and progressive. Even though my profile was at its peak, the majority of my paid opportunities had gone away, with brands deeming me too controversial to work with. This was a time before most mainstream brands were willing to confidently take a stand on 'politically divisive' topics such as LGBTQ rights and racism – with the extent of brand support often consisting of sticking a rainbow flag on a product as a sign of solidarity, even though the proceeds still went to the company. Speaking about racism, on the other hand, was considered strictly a no-go area, as per my predicament.

Since then, how we talk about the symptoms of oppression has gone mainstream, but talking about them on social media has its limits. Increasingly, I think we need to migrate from it back to real life. Certain disadvantages of social media are often discussed: the capacity for mob mentality, the ease in which misinformation can spread, the way we all live in our own bubbles, the way we grow tribal, refusing to engage with people who hold different views as one might in real life. A disproportionate amount of airtime is dedicated to cancellation by people who've never previously experienced anyone disagreeing with them. I think things like 'cancel culture', call-out culture and pile-ons are sometimes necessary to draw attention to things. But I don't believe this is going to be enough for change. Social media companies aren't built to overthrow systemic oppression; they uphold it within the very functioning of their platforms. In addition to this, billionaires are not the people who are about to hand us the tools to overthrow power structures that they benefit from. Mark Zuckerberg, Elon Musk and ByteDance are not about to liberate us. The algorithmic functioning of social media companies simply isn't built for marginalised people because at large they are not coded by people with marginalised experiences.

In the 2020 documentary *Coded Bias*, computer scientist Joy Buolamwini explores how bias is heavily coded into facial-recognition software, algorithms and machine learning. She emphasises how unregulated the field is when it comes to racism, inaccuracy or unintentional impact. Buolamwini's interest in this area began when she realised as part of her own studies that the facial-recognition programme she was using wouldn't recognise her own face, as a Black woman. But when she held a white mask up to her face, it would be recognised instantly.

Joy later went on to find that facial-recognition software works 99 per cent of the time when the person is a white man, but errors in identification are 35 per cent more likely to happen when the person is a darker-skinned woman. According to an article by Steve Lohr in the *New York Times*, 'in modern artificial intelligence data rules. A.I. software is only as smart as the data used to train it. If there are many more white men than Black women in the system, it will be worse at identifying the Black women.' *WIRED* reported that only 12 per cent of leading machine-learning researchers are female, 15 per cent of Artificial Intelligence researchers at Meta are female and at Google it's just 10 per cent.

The vast majority of the people coding the algorithms that impact our daily lives are cis white men, resulting in those algorithms reflecting and upholding the way those men see the world as a priority. The way that certain users are prioritised within a feed is impacted by algorithms; what is flagged as restricted content is impacted by algorithms. Algorithms play a massive part in not only what is presented to us online, but how we are presented to others. We need to transition away from our dependence on and addiction to Silicon Valley, especially when it comes to wanting to enact real lasting change. No one's going to break out of the glass house while we're all still in it. The virtual world can at best only ever be part of our toolkit and it cannot be sustainably relied on as a medium for activism or as an ally to our causes. I'm not saying that we should all commit to a mass exodus and leave these apps behind and go back to a life before smartphones. But we do need to be aware of how the programming of the platforms that many of us are addicted to and rely on professionally, is, at its core, built out of an unequal view of the world, heavily skewed in favour of a white patriarchal cisgender mindset.

*

I think the best way to view activism is as a machine, built of different parts with different functions that all interact to allow it to work effectively and efficiently. Activist organisations need organisers, but also bookkeepers, public speakers, writers, fundraisers, researchers, allies, ambassadors, artists and lawyers. There are so many different facets to activism. It really relies on people using their expertise as individuals and giving what they can to fight for a communal cause. Activism is about waking people up and shaking the table; it's about empowering people to empower other people, to identify the issue and approach it from new angles.

We need to transition as a society into a more open-minded people, who are capable of championing or at least hearing out unpopular voices who question ingrained systems of power and privilege. For instance, a lot of us were initially uncomfortable or confused at the thought of defunding the police. It's difficult to envision society functioning in a way that transcends what we have always known. We all felt horror when we read the news of Sarah Everard's murder at the hands of London Metropolitan police officer Wayne Couzens, and we'd heard the idea before, coming from activists in America, but still, defunding the police feels too radical for many – doesn't that spell anarchy?

No, not at all. I don't believe that most people who shudder at the thought of defunding the police know how policing is funded and organised. The contemporary police force was never built to serve a progressive, diverse society. Its foundations come from a time when the police existed to protect certain bodies and punish others. Again, this is not a matter of a few bad apples: racism, homophobia, ableism and sexism are built-in. Perhaps this will be the next conversation we'll be willing to have when, once more, something unthinkable happens and demands the attention of the mainstream. But the conversation will only happen when we all grow comfortable or at least capable of confronting our own beliefs. To truly engage with these concepts, we have to open ourselves to the discomfort of feeling them, to make the effort to look for information on them rather than relying on social media nuggets – we have to educate ourselves on the possibilities of what a new world could look like, before writing it off as fantasy. Isn't everything just a fantasy before it's achieved? Isn't that the whole point of innovation and change, the ability to make dreams of progress a reality? I don't think you can truly claim to be part of progress without understanding that you yourself might subconsciously be resisting change.

I started out building a public platform because I wanted to be a representative for my community; I wanted to speak about things that weren't being spoken about; I wanted to be the change I hadn't seen before. It's been thirteen years now since I stared my transgender journey and those parts of myself have at times started to feel like they have become the whole of my identity in the eyes of other people. The downside with public-facing activism is the expectation that comes with it, that everything that you do has to be related to the 'issue' that concerns you.

I've been working in the fashion and beauty space in the public eye for eight years and although I have seen the industry change in phenomenal ways and am proud have played a small part in that change, we still have so far to go. For a lot of my career, because I was often the first trans person to achieve certain things, I've felt like I had to be perfect to be taken seriously. I've often ended up being referred to as a role model, while being unsure of whether I could ever truly live up to such an accolade.

Facing the pressure of being the first trans person in British history to get such massive opportunities within the fashion and beauty industry, such as being the first trans model to work with L'Oréal, the first British Black trans woman on the cover of British *Vogue* or the first trans woman on the cover of *Cosmopolitan* UK, is often as anxiety-inducing as it is affirming. There's been immense pressure to get everything right, not just for myself; I felt that if I got it wrong, I would have given people the excuse they were looking for to not hire others like me, and that I would justify their bigotry. It's great to be in the room now but the reality that I am currently navigating is one not entirely representative of the realities of most trans people in the UK, or for that matter, the world. I do struggle with finding my way through this very newly gained privilege of access, finance, safety and employment because I don't want it to mould me into somebody that I no longer recognise.

A glamorous industry saying they stand behind the trans community, with often only my personal success to show for it, stopped feeling real or genuine a long time ago – even if it is genuine, it's not enough. It wasn't enough when I was the only one and it's still not enough now with only a handful of us in the room. At times I've felt like I've been co-opted by brands, but I've let it happen because I had to survive a very public life on an income that didn't mirror that of my cisgender peers, but with outgoings and expenses that did.

I've found myself censoring what I say, censoring my ideas, often questioning whether it would be seen as appropriate for an employer. I've realised that it isn't possible to stand up for every single issue that I care about, even though I'm often expected to, because I am just one person. For a long while I felt great pride and joy in being able to represent and create greater visibility for my community, even though at times situations left me feeling used. After a while though, you look at yourself and think, 'Who even am I?', 'Is this even authentic to me or am I now just performing myself for the sake of being visible?' I've started to wonder if there might be other, more authentic ways of being, of working. I was beginning to feel like I was assimilating myself into the mainstream, internalising the pressure to be the palatable face of Black trans women in the UK.

I have no desire for my transness to be rendered unspoken but I do find it frustrating how little opportunity there is for trans people within the industry – in fields that don't revolve around gender, sexuality and identity. It would be great if a trans person could be given a platform, could be asked to be involved in a project just for being good at what they do, or because they have an interest in that specific area.

It's twice the work when you have to do your job plus having to talk about everything this represents. My cisgender peers manage to get the same types of jobs as me without having to lead discussions about their identity with every job they book. We've established that cisgender women don't want to have to talk about being women *all the time*, so why should we? But it seems that we are often still not invited into these spaces without our difference being harnessed as a selling point. These conversations are necessary but I'm beginning to despair as to when or whether we're ever going to get past this. Are minorities only going to be included as an act of representation or can we move this needle forward to actual inclusion?

It's not activism I want to step away from. It's the feeling of expectation that has begun to feel heavy. It's the feeling of having to do it on other people's terms, in ways that no longer feel like the progress that I want to see for society or for myself. I don't want to be hyper-present on social media, I don't want to share my every waking thought on every issue. I don't want to fall into the trap of performing parts of me for others, at the expense of living a life of wholeness that feels good for myself.

★

I think I'm tired of chaos and would like some peace now. I've come to realise that I've always lived within the parameters of chaos – the internal chaos of my childhood became the external chaos of nightlife, which later became the chaos of the media. When the pandemic hit, even though my life was objectively positive in so many ways, I found myself experiencing panic attacks and uncontrollable racing thoughts. I was free of the external chaos for the first time, everything was on pause and with no distractions, so I experienced all the trauma that I had stored and suppressed in my body over the years.

From being targeted in the street to being targeted by members of the House of Lords, to being verbally assaulted on live television, to being raped, my abusive relationships, my resentment over my childhood with my father, my experiences of self-harm and anorexia, all rose up in one go. I was angry with everything and everyone. I was having night sweats and paralysing episodes in which I couldn't breathe and would begin hyperventilating. As soon as it became possible to travel, I went on holiday. While there I booked myself into rehab on my return.

It was then that I realised that I was experiencing symptoms of complex PTSD. I had grown furious at my parents again and was fixated on the idea of what could have been if I hadn't had to navigate my way through my childhood. I had found it so difficult to heal because so much of my career has been moulded around my experiences. So much of how I saw myself was in such close proximity to my trauma. I started to think about how I could leave this behind and transition into the next stage of my life. My trip to rehab feels like the beginning of the new era for me. I want to live a life in which I can exist outside of my trauma rather than letting it define me. I want to heal.

Sometimes I wish I could go back in time as an encouraging adult and tell my younger self that I will one day be the embodiment of my wildest dreams – but in order to make them a reality and be happy, I have to be on my own side. I wish I could tell younger me that one day I'd not only be on the cover of that British *Vogue* that I was reading while hiding in the school toilets, but I'd also be on the masthead as a contributing editor. I'd also be the first trans woman to make the cover of *Cosmopolitan*, in the same year. I wish I could tell younger me to hold on to those dreams, that they are possible for someone like me, and that I would also be the one to make those dreams easier for others to achieve.

Trauma keeps us chained to the past. It wasn't until I sat down and relived some of the most difficult moments of my life while writing this book, that I realised how hard I have found it to move on, how hard I have found it to forgive, how hesitant I sometimes am to embrace uncertainty and personal change and how much I have defined myself by what I have been through rather than what I am capable of.

This process has helped me to realise that while my trauma has shaped both me and my past actions, it doesn't need to shape my future. I won't allow it the power to do so any more.

Instead of being angry at the individuals whose actions have caused me pain, I have realised that a better use of my energy and my purpose is to refocus it on the societal systems that allowed that harm to take place. I'm angry at the systemic queerphobia and societal stigmas that are tearing families apart, stopping parents from seeing their kids in their wholeness and allowing them to be their true selves, robbing them of childhoods they can look back on and draw power from in later life.

Rebuilding a relationship with my parents has been one of the most necessary, rewarding and healing processes in my recovery. The concept of forgiveness has often eluded me. Historically I have preferred to choose to forget, whether by suppressing difficult memories, blocking myself from feeling certain emotions or pretending that those who had wronged me no longer existed. Whether I wanted to admit it or not, denial has often been my go-to strategy in the pursuit of happiness and self-preservation. But denial is not a sustainable tactic. Sooner or later you have to face the music if you want to move on and heal, rather than run away while carrying the unconscious weight of it with you.

I still don't agree with the way that my father treated me as a child, but today, neither does he. It's far more nourishing to my inner child and my adult soul for us to heal together, rather than to continue the hurt of estrangement. I don't want that for myself, I don't want that for my future children or for my potential grandchildren. Similarly, I don't agree with my mother's reaction to my coming out when I was younger, but now neither does she, so instead I choose to be proud of her for how far she has come, to allow her to be proud of who I have become and for us to continue to grow together.

We cannot fully heal with one foot in the past and the other in the present. We cannot move forward without freeing ourselves from how the past made us feel at the time. Sooner or later, healing has to happen and forgiveness has to ensue to change how we feel right now. But it has to happen on a common ground, and I can't tell you how happy I am that we have found ours.

It's taken a long time for me to recognise that I am the one in the driving seat of my life, that I have the wheel right in front of me and I don't need permission to grasp it with both hands to take it where I want to go as a primary intention rather than a reaction. As corny as it may sound, I've come to realise that happiness cannot remain a goal situated at a destination. It can't be rooted in 'if only'; if only I move to this city, if only

I get this surgery, if only I meet this partner, if only I achieve this accolade, *if only, if only, if only* – there will always be another *if only* once we realise that the previous one didn't fix what we are running from – ourselves. Happiness isn't over there, it's in the here and now. It has to be now, and we are the source.

I don't want to define myself by the negative events or mistakes of my past, so defining others by theirs – especially when they also display the intention to grow and heal – serves no one; it just continues the pain and trauma for us both. Humans are imperfect by design, and accepting that others haven't always been the best version of themselves is part of recognising that neither have I; it's a process that we all endure. I'm choosing to bond with others in that imperfection and willingness to change, rather than gatekeep the growth for myself in denying them forgiveness or understanding.

I want to plug into myself and discover more about who I am right now and what I can bring to the table going forward. I have every intention of thriving, of showing people what a woman like me can do. That's my activism of self, realising who I am and changing the boundaries of what I want to achieve. What I do know for sure is that everything changes. No one stays the same for ever. In one way or another, we all transition.

Acknowledgements

Mum

In writing this book, I have realised that I was at times an utter, absolute and complete nightmare to raise, I hope that this book somewhat helps to further clarify as to why – thank you for your love and understanding despite it all. Our road hasn't always been smooth or linear, but amongst the sink holes, diversions and oil spills we made it to where we are today. Thank you for all you sacrificed for me, for how stern you were with me, for how you always encouraged me to aim just that bit higher even when I didn't know what I was reaching for. I get it now. I get it.

Dad

All I ever wanted was to one day make you and Mum proud. I'm so glad we pushed through and made it to the other side. The past is the past and we've both grown so much. Thank you for all of your support, even when you don't completely understand what I'm doing or going on about. I'm proud to say that we are proof that sometimes it really is all okay in the end. I love this place that we are in, how we have held space for each other to grow and see each other with new eyes, free of judgement and open wide to each other as we are.

Simon

I'm sorry for the chaos, I was in pain. I know you understand but I also want you to know how much I appreciate your patience and support. Coming out to you as gay and then later as trans were two of the easiest 'coming outs' that I've ever experienced. I'm so proud of you, your journey and the person you've become. Keep living boldly and on your own terms. Sending you love across the Atlantic.

Felix

I love you so much, and seemingly more so every time I see you smile. Thank you for loving the wholeness of me, for showing me that I don't need to hide the messy parts of myself to be seen as loveable. I always feel both at home and on holiday whenever I'm with you. I love us, beyond borders. The smartest, most talented, interesting, beautiful, wise, charming, fun and charismatic man I know, also happens to be my man. I lucked the fuck out. My Pisces King!

Reece

My soulmate, best friend, future baby daddy, rock, confidant and hypeman. I cannot imagine life without you. We share so many incredible memories, highs and lows. I love you downnnn. Thank you for being such a bright light in my life. Thank you for being there for me throughout some of the most impossible moments. I'm always here for you.

Tommy

At this point we're family. The big brother I never had, the worst influence in my phonebook and the most loyal friend in the world. Thank you for being there even when I made it close to impossible. Our friendship is so precious to me, a truly unbreakable bond.

Dr Jess Moriarty

I'm convinced that you may be my guardian angel. I can't say thank you enough for helping me make it through those challenging university years. Thank you for just listening, for holding up a mirror and urging me to make life work for me. The impact you had on me and the tools you helped me develop during those difficult years prepared me for my life and career today, and for that I'm eternally grateful. Thank you. Thank you. Thank you. I hope your current students know how lucky they are!

Bergstrom Studio

Abigail, you have the mind of a genius and the patience of a saint. Thank you for being the most incredible literary agent, for supporting me through this entire project and for helping me to believe in myself and my abilities, even when I missed pretty much every deadline – oops! It is an absolute joy working with you. Without you, none of this would have been possible. Thank you!

Bloomsbury & HarperCollins

Alexis and Rakesh, it means so much to me that you believed in my vision for this book from the get go, that you saw the value in my story and understood why it should be told. I'm so proud of what we have created together and I'm so excited to share it with the world. This has been a real labour of love and pain, it's taken time, sweat and tears, but we did it! Thank you for your support, patience and guidance over the past three years.

Diving Bell Group

Justin and Kim, my day ones! You are two of the most phenomenal people I know. Thank you for believing in me when it felt like the industry had written me off. Thank you for constantly challenging yourselves to grow, as well as me. Thank you for building an agency that centres purpose and positive change as its driving force. I'm so proud to not only be managed by you both, but also to call you my close friends. What a journey we have been on.

Satellite 414

Tom and Lottie, what an absolute dream team you are. Thank you for ever raising the bar, for your encouragement and for always having every situation handled. Working with you both is an absolute joy. Best publicists in the game.

A Note on the Author

Munroe Bergdorf is an internationally renowned activist, model, writer and broadcaster. She was appointed as Contributing Editor at British *Vogue*, and has contributed to publications including the *Guardian*, *Evening Standard*, *Grazia*, *i-D*, *Elle*, *Teen Vogue* and *Paper*.

In 2019, Bergdorf was awarded an honorary doctorate for campaigning for transgender rights by the University of Brighton, and appointed as a National Advocate for UN Women UK. Munroe is a proud ambassador for gender variant and transgender youth charity Mermaids and a founding consultant of L'Oreal Paris's UK Diversity and Inclusion Board. She has also spoken at international institutions from Oxford University to the UN General Assembly.

Munroe is the host of the critically acclaimed podcast *The Way We Are* on Spotify and fronts the hit MTV show *Queerpiphany*. Her first film, *What Makes a Woman*, premiered on Channel 4 in 2018.

A Note on the Type

The text of this book is set in Bembo, which was first used in 1495 by the Venetian printer Aldus Manutius for Cardinal Bembo's *De Aetna*. The original types were cut for Manutius by Francesco Griffo. Bembo was one of the types used by Claude Garamond (1480–1561) as a model for his Romain de l'Université, and so it was a forerunner of what became the standard European type for the following two centuries. Its modern form follows the original types and was designed for Monotype in 1929.